Self Active Play

Awakens **Creativity**
Empowers **Self Discovery**
Inspires **Optimism**

WALTER F. DREW, Ed.D. & MARCIA L. NELL, Ph.D.

Other books by the authors:
From Play to Practice:
Connecting Teachers' Play to Children's Learning
Published by: The National Association for the Education of Young Children

Published by
Institute for Self Active Education, Inc.
Melbourne Beach, Florida
www.isaeplay.org

Cover design by
BRC60.com
Merritt Island, FL

Text format by
Sticky Earth Books
Exton, Pennsylvania

Paperback ISBN: 978-1-7368773-0-2

To Terri with love Walter

DEDICATION

For Kitty, my amazing wife, artist and founding partner of the Institute for Self Active Education, for your steadfast love and dearest friendship which sustains the spirit of this play work, for my fantastic children, Benjamin, Gita, Sarita, Elijah John, Terri, Mark and Jason, for my children's spouses Molly, Tracy and Cesar, for my gifted grandchildren, Owen, Aidan, Hannah Lee, John Henry and Sopris, for my brother Bob, for the love and inspiration you all share with me and one another, I dedicate this book to you, heart of my family.

Walter

This book is dedicated to my husband, Thomas. His love and support have made my life's journey so interesting! I appreciate his sense of adventure, creativity, and strong work ethic. Thank you for living life with me. I also, would like to dedicate this book to my children (Carrie, Michelle, Lucas, & Justin), their spouses (Ted, David, Esther, & Laura), and my grandchildren (Bryce, Nic, Lee & all the new ones on the way). Each one has brought such joy, happiness and inspiration to keep moving forward. Thank you!

Marcia

Table of Contents

PART II

PART III

ACKNOWLEDGMENTS

We would like to acknowledge our esteemed colleagues who have shared their inspired thoughts and experiences in this book, which provides the reader with a deeper and richer context and importance of self active play.

In chapter 2, Shariee Calderone shared her perspective in the section entitled, *Applying the Principles: Expanding the Conscious Awareness of Play with Adults*. Dr. Sean Durham, assistant professor at Auburn University, provided reflective insight into his own self active play experience in the section *Professor's Reflection*.

In chapter 3, Pre-K teacher Ellen Grogan shared how she introduced self active play with her children and the important outcomes realized through quiet play with open-ended materials. Art Hoelke and Valerie Ryan, two business leaders, describe their perspectives on how businesses can support children's creative development. Sue Blandford, Founding Director of the St. Louis Teachers Recycle Center, shares how play with simple materials awakens imagination and creative thought. Also, in this chapter, Paola Lopez, founder and president of the Kinderoo Children's Academy in Ocala, Florida, describes the essential value of materials in nurturing and transforming the professional practices of her teachers.

In chapter 4, Early Childhood Specialists, Michelle Compton & Beth Severson of the Manatee County Public Schools in Florida described in detail the process and results of applying hands-on professional development play training with a group of early childhood educators and the resultant improvement in classroom practices.

In chapter 5, Dr. James Johnson, professor at The Pennsylvania State University, wrote about the importance of mixed age play in his section entitled *Reflections on Mixed-Age Play in Theory and*

Practice. Also, in chapter 5, Maria Christina and Edward Pazzanese shared their award-winning efforts of providing community-based play and art making experiences in the section *The Story: Families Playing and Creating Art Together.*

Chapter 6 has a riveting account by Dr. Fraser Brown about his work with children in his section *Restoring Hope Through Play-Therapeutic Playwork in Transylvania.* Also in Chapter 6, Terri Drew presents how *Contemplative Self Active Play* is used in palliative care as an integrative practice in meeting persons where they are for the facilitation of self-actualization and wellbeing.

Then in Chapter 7, Dr. Michael Patte, Professor of Teaching and Learning from Bloomsburg University in Pennsylvania wrote about his work with pre-service teachers, *Preparing Future Teachers for Play Advocacy.* Dr. Michael Wragg, Senior Lecturer at Leeds Beckett University, School of Health and Community Studies in the United Kingdom shared his thoughts in *Play and Prosperity.*

We would like to thank each one of our colleagues for their thoughtful work and their willingness to share those thoughts in this book.

FORWARD

As a long-time supporter of the Institute for Self-Active Education and a participant in several of its play workshops, I am very pleased to see this book, which describes the Institute's theoretical foundations, research commitments, and practical recommendations for persons wishing to explore the meanings of play in schools, businesses, and communities.

To speak of play workshops may seem a contradiction in terms, as many people hold the view that work and play are opposites. Champions of what I call constructive play, the authors demonstrate that processes of making, such as building freely with material objects or creating works of art, are at their best avenues of self-discovery.

In that spirit, they describe the methods they have developed over the years to create welcoming play spaces that honor the free expression of players, encourage their focus on the matters at hand, promote their personal reflection and sharing, and otherwise encourage them to develop communities that respect the contributions of all. Those lessons—about the importance of collective as well as personal experience, the significance of meditation and listening in creative endeavors, and the prospects for diversely situated persons to establish supportive relationships through play—are of crucial importance to people at every stage of the life cycle.

The authors direct themselves especially to the educators of young children, who wish to incorporate a new style of play into their classrooms. However, play advocates addressing the needs of senior citizens in assisted living centers, emotionally withdrawn persons, fragmented communities, and dysfunctional organizations also will benefit greatly from reading this book.

Thomas S. Henricks

Author of *Play and the Human Condition* (2016)
and *Play: A Basic Pathway to the Self* (2020)

INTRODUCTION

"The object, which is in back of every true work of art, is the attainment of a state of being, a state of high functioning, a more than ordinary moment of existence. In such moments activity is inevitable, and whether this activity is with brush, pen, chisel or tongue, its result is but a by-product of the state, a trace, the footprint of the state."

—Robert Henri, (1923, p. 157)

FIRST AND FOREMOST, the groundwork of self active play is rooted in the awareness that play in the early years is an essential developmentally appropriate practice necessary for healthy human development and continues across the entire life span. Whether as a child or an adult, self active play puts the player in control of the experience, free to create and express their unique thoughts and feelings.

Our desire is to share insights and details about how others are developing, practicing, and expanding upon self active play. Self active play uses open-ended materials in hands-on silent solitary and cooperative play experiences. Each format is designed to awaken creativity and self-expression in children and adults alike. Self active play maximizes freedom, self-directed learning, and creative problem solving related to the individual's personal interests. Our vision is to see the world filled with self active play that awakens the creative spirit and encourages self-discovery, imagination, and wonderment in people everywhere.

Self active play is an extraordinary means of educating adults about the complexity and the critical role of play in healthy human development, especially in the lives of children. Just as with children, play informs and inspires adults with essential mindfulness, relevant insight, imagination, and pure enjoyment. As we focus and fiddle with open-ended materials, we re-establish what Froebel calls "inner connection", a source of peace, wisdom, and healing. It isn't only the child that benefits from self active play.

The stories and images in this book reveal how self active play exerts a profound influence on creating, inventing, and discovering who we are, what we feel, and who we become. In sharing our work with you, we acknowledge all the play leaders who have come before us and who travel with us now. Much of our philosophy and foundational belief system is built upon the work of our play forefathers, especially Friedrich Froebel and Brian Sutton-Smith. We also rely heavily on the works of current play scholars, including Thomas Henricks, Stuart Brown, and Peter Gray, who continue to inform and inspire our self active play practices. We further acknowledge all of the participants who engaged their hands, hearts, and minds in play workshops and willingly shared their personal stories, insights, and understandings through their play journal reflections, interviews, and focus group discussions.

We are grateful to the groundbreaking work of the Institute for Self Active Education (ISAE) established in Boston by Walter and Kitty Drew in 1980 as a 501(c) 3 nonprofit organization. The mission of ISAE is to awaken the creative potential of children and adults through hands-on self active play and art making with open-ended materials.

OUR PURPOSE

OUR FIRST PURPOSE in writing this book is to present a simple research-based process that promotes a deeper conscious awareness of play and how it generates self-awareness, self-understanding, and self-realization. This simple self active play process uses open-ended materials to stimulate the curiosity and active engagement of the player that results in creative discovery learning, social emotional wellbeing and inner peace. We hope that this work continues through the efforts of our youthful, playful compatriots.

Dr. Peter Gray states, "Children are designed, by nature, to play and explore on their own, independently of adults. They need freedom in order to develop; without it they suffer. The desire to play freely is a basic, biological drive. Lack of free play may not kill the physical body, as would lack of food, air, or water, but it kills the spirit and stunts mental growth" (Gray 2013, 4–5). As Gray suggests, when children are not provided with opportunities to participate in free, open-ended play, they *suffer*.

Our second purpose in writing this book is to present research-based evidence to support the use of self active play as a way of positively influencing children's growth, development, and well-being. The goal is for children to grow into playful, healthy, happy adults, who have a lasting desire to continue playing throughout their lives and to pass that culture of play on to younger generations.

A third purpose is to provide effective play-based tools to strengthen advocacy efforts. Teachers often wonder how to convey to families and administrators why play is imperative for children. We cite abundant research supporting the use of self active play and share examples of how teachers and school systems are actively using self active play to create a play-friendly culture. The goal is to inspire more play advocates to be ready, willing, and able to include self active play in their professional practice with children, teachers, families, and administrators who wish to see children thrive.

Our fourth purpose is to highlight the important role business and industry play by donating their excess by-products, overruns and reject materials that are used in the self active play process. In large part, the mission of ISAE has been successful due to the generous donation of these materials to local recycle and reusable resource centers, which make the materials available for use in self active play. Art Hoelke, is a businessman who has contributed materials extensively to a reusable resource center.

Business-education partnerships of this kind are a natural, cost-effective, environmentally conscious way to strengthen quality early learning through creative play. This book shows how byproducts, overruns, and outdated materials provided by local industries are being used in Head Start classrooms, family education programs, college classrooms, professional development workshops, and centers serving children suffering from sudden traumatic loss. Our hope is that more leaders in business and industry see the connection between their excess material donations and the development of a more qualified, successful workforce.

The fifth purpose for writing this book is to encourage self active play across the entire human life span. Given play awakens creativity and strengthens resilience in older adults play improves the Quality of Life by enhancing vitality, spontaneity, and a zest for life. Just as with young children, play sparks imagination, creativity, optimism and sense of emotional well-being as adults age. The adaptive variability of self-active play makes it a unique and enjoyable universal process safe and appropriate for all ages.

THE JOURNEY

THIS BOOK OUTLINES the theory, principles, and components of self active play.

In Chapter 1 we look at the researchers who have created the foundation upon which self active play firmly stands.

In Chapter 2 we lay out the seven principles of self active play and the powerful role of play in education and human development.

Chapter 3 explores the essential elements and materials of the self active play process, the role of the adult in children's self active play, and the two basic types of self active play experiences: solo and cooperative play.

Chapter 4 is an in-depth case study of how self active play was used as a structured protocol for improving science education with Pre-teachers serving in classroom within the public system of Manatee County, Florida.

Chapter 5 highlights the use of self active play with older adults, including in intergenerational play, assisted-living facilities, and mixed-age-group play. These specific stories illuminate the far-reaching benefits of self active play throughout the human lifespan.

Chapter 6 features the restorative power of play applied in four therapeutic settings. The first story concerns severely neglected children in Romania. The second story is about a Medical-Surgical Unit in a community hospital in California. The third example refers to a clinical nursing program in a long term care facility, also in California. The last application involves the restorative power of play in a community program for children and families suffering from sudden traumatic loss in Melbourne, Florida.

Chapter 7, discusses the ideas of advocacy and resiliency offering a glimpse into a country that has a culture of play. We explore an advocacy strategy to foster the growth and development of a culture that is supportive of play across the life cycle.

We include original contributions from five prominent play theorists: Thomas Henricks, James Johnson, Fraser Brown, Michael Patte, and Michael Wragg. These new writings discuss the promise of play, mixed-age play, therapeutic play, pop-up adventure playgrounds, and play and prosperity. We are grateful for their time and pleased to add their expertise in support of expanding opportunities for children and adults to engage in self active play.

We share our own stories and those of many others who have joined us on the journey of self active play, including commentaries from various practicing early childhood teachers. Throughout the book, these professionals' experiences with self active play are set apart and presented in their own words.

PART I

THEORY OF
SELF ACTIVE PLAY
EDUCATION

Chapter 1

Theoretical Foundation of Self Active Play

"Spontaneous efforts. But what the teacher presents does not always absorb the whole attention, sometimes not at all. The child has its own interests. Some knowledge it strongly desires, and therefore will seek this of its own free will and throw its whole soul into the search. The will, stimulated by self-activity of all the faculties, prompts to spontaneous efforts. This is a step toward moral self-activity and independence."

—Johann Heinrich Pestalozzi, (1898, p. 12)

PLAY HAS FASCINATED and captured the attention of humans across time, cultures, and species. Plato, in his work *The Republic,* states that *"youth is the time of study, and here we must remember that the mind is free and dainty, and, unlike the body, must not be made to work against the grain. Learning should be at first a sort of play, in which the natural bent is detected"* (2017, 117). Plato recognized that play was a natural state for young children and that adults should recognize it as an asset in children's learning.

Researchers likewise recognize play as a universal state of being in both children and adults. Erik Erikson, for example, created the term "transcen*dance*," a way of "regaining lost skills, including play, activity, joy . . . a major leap above and beyond the fear of death" (1997, 127). Erikson advocated for the necessity of play across the human life cycle, especially in old age, and showed the value of play across the life span as a useful and vital tool as he contemplated his own life.

This chapter considers human play from multiple perspectives and in multiple sources. Each of the influential researchers reviewed provide a foundational pillar of self active play that helps to lay the groundwork for understanding its significance.

Friedrich Froebel, *The Education of Man*

"By education, then, the divine essence of man should be unfolded, brought out, lifted into consciousness, and man himself raised into free, conscious obedience to the divine principle that lives in him, and to a free representation of this principle in his life."

—Friedrich Froebel, (2005, p. 4-5).

Friedrich Froebel, known as the "Father of Kindergarten", has had a tremendous influence on those who work with young children. Froebel stressed the importance of children being self active in the learning process. According to Froebel, children sensorily engage in pattern play and construction with wooden blocks, bits of yarn, or little wooden sticks. Learning, according to Froebel, places the child at the center: it is not just the external experience happening *to* children but also includes the internal understandings *of* the children. Unlike other philosophers, he viewed children as capable and filled with powerful internal understandings that need to be shared with others. The expression of what children understand or see as they plan and learn is therefore vital in the educational process.

One example of the relationship between external objects and children's internal response to the experiences is when a four-year-old girl lays bits of blue silk fabric on a white piece of mat board, then places small red and yellow plastic caps around the fabric, and then looks up and says, "This is the river that runs behind my house." The outer form expressed with the materials is a representation of the child's internal response to her silent self active play. External and internal experiences influence each other. As a vital and vibrant participant in learning, the child is "self active" in her educational pursuits and creates within herself a "habit of success, a calm sense of power, a firm conviction of mastership" (Froebel 2005, 37).

According to Froebel, "play is the highest phase of child development" (54). It promotes "joy, freedom, contentment, inner and outer rest and peace with the world," and a child who participates wholeheartedly in self active play experiences "will surely be a thorough, determined man [or woman], capable of self-sacrifice for the promotion of the welfare of himself [or herself] and others" (55). Froebel described play as "not trivial, it is highly serious and of deep significance" (55) and as humans' "first poetical (creative) utterance" (58).

Froebel was a strong proponent of putting children at the center of their own education. Along with this child-centered perspective, Froebel stressed the importance of children being fully active in their learning. Many of today's educational methods would not meet his criteria for appropriate educational techniques. He stressed the value of using materials to solidify the connection between the external and internal worlds. Froebel recognized the internal world of the child as an important aspect in the learning process. He also emphasized the importance of play as a means for children to discover meaning from the external world and to connect that meaning to their internal worlds; the reciprocal nature of these two worlds promote self-discovery.

Stuart Brown with Christopher Vaughn,

Play: How it Shapes the Brain, Opens the Imagination, and Invigorates the Soul

> *"Nothing lights up a child's brain like play."*
>
> —Stuart Brown, (2016, p. 10)

Stuart Brown is a well-known medical doctor and trained psychiatrist. His fascination with the study of play began early in his career, when he was asked to do a psychiatric evaluation of Charles Whitman, the man responsible for the University of Texas watchtower sniper attack on August 1, 1966, in Austin, Texas. As a young assistant professor of psychiatry at Baylor College of Medicine, Brown was asked by his department chair to work with Governor John Connally of Texas to discover why people were predisposed to these kinds of violent acts and how to identify them. Answering this pressing question was a focal point of Brown's early work.

In an interview with the shooter, Brown found that Whitman had an overbearing father who abused his mother in his presence. But Brown discovered another compelling factor: Whitman lacked play experiences throughout his life. Whitman's overcontrolled childhood led to outward conformity but internal turmoil. The typical self-understanding a child gains through play, such as freedom of choice and a sense of safety, were underdeveloped in Whitman, and his lack of play experiences manifested in his inability to make decisions for himself. Brown clearly understood the consequences of play deprivation. When looking at other adults who had been deprived of rich play experiences as children, he realized that the costs to typical development are quite profound. He continued his study of the effects of play deprivation and how it contributes to deep-seated psychopathology and also investigated the many benefits linked to rich play lives.

Play has been espoused to promote many benefits, but what is play, exactly? How do we know it when we see it or experience it? According to Brown and Vaughn (2015, 17) play consists of seven properties.

1. Play is *purposeless.*

It does not have an outside value beyond itself. This sense of purposelessness sets play apart from many other life activities.

2. Play must be *voluntary.*

It has to be chosen by the player; you can't tell someone to play.

3. Play has an *inherent attraction.*

In other words, play is fun! It invites the player to participate again and again.

4. Play invokes *no sense of time.*

It releases players from the reality of time, and they get lost in the play.

5. Play creates a *loss of the sense of self.*

Players can assume any role. Mihaly Csikszentmihalyi (1996) described this property as "flow," where one loses oneself in the midst of the moment.

6. Play has a sense of the *spontaneous or improvisational.*

The possibilities are framed by the bounds of one's imagination. In other words, the sky's the limit—sometimes quite literally.

7. Play evokes *continuation desire.*

It warrants a return to sustain or persist in the action or state of being.

When these seven properties are present in an experience, then it can be said to be play.

The results of Brown's studies emphasize the importance of play to healthy development for young children. In play, children are able to freely manipulate the play experience and to maneuver beyond normal constraints, creating a sense of freedom, wonderment, and imagination. At the same time, children understand and know that the situation is indeed play and therefore is something that can be altered, especially if a sense of discomfort arises. By having the ability to make these decisions on their own, children develop a clearer understanding of themselves, their self-efficacy, and their ability to manipulate situations that affect their lives.

Brown also expressed the vital need for children to better acquaint themselves with their own inner wants, needs, and desires through play (105). Through play, children create a clearer understanding of what kinds of activities excite them, nurture their curiosity, and stimulate their inner motivation. This self-knowledge permeates the child's life span. Play also provides a context in which children come to terms with opposing factions from within. For example, during play the "head" may tell children to go in one direction while the "heart" suggests another. Children find a balance between these two factions via the experimentation that occurs in their play. Many researchers cite finding internal motivational inspirations and self-control throughout the life span as one of play's major contributions.

Brown also warned of the overscheduling of children and their need to be their own directors of circumstances (105). Many children are involved in so many adult-directed and -organized activities that their sense of freedom and their own preferences are not nurtured. During play, children develop a sense of what they like and what they prefer to do. And sometimes, doing *nothing* is just what they need! Brown stated that the children's choices and freedom to select activities provided insight to the children about their own preferences and ultimately allowed them to access and develop their own sense of motivation.

Brown further asserted that the impulse to play is actually a biological drive, such as the need for food, water, and shelter. This biological need does not diminish over time but remains throughout the lifespan, so play still provides valuable benefits to adults. *Play in work* as a concept has been disputed by many scholars as an oxymoron, but Brown continues to assert that it is the play element present in work that helps adults to make sense of their world and incorporating play into work can bring about a transformation, lending a newness to the work that was not there before. Many of the difficulties faced in work require clear thinking, a high degree of problem solving, and a new way of looking at a situation: that is, creativity. The connection between play and work is the creative ability to see new connections and possibilities through a different lens. This new perspective builds new understandings, meanings, and possibilities. For Brown, the opposite of play is not work, but depression (126). He stated that "the most significant aspect of play is that it allows us to express our joy" (218). Strong play experiences in childhood thus support strong adult development.

Thomas S. Henricks, *Play and the Human Condition*

"How do we discover who we are? How do we determine the character of the world in which we live? And how do we decide what we can do in a world so configured?"

—Henricks, (2015, 1)

Dr. Henricks asked questions such as these and connected them to play and the quest for self-realization. His book *Play and the Human Condition* provides a framework for understanding the diverse perspectives on and theoretical underpinnings of the study of play. By acknowledging, categorizing, and articulating these perspectives, he enables readers to clearly comprehend the complexity of play and suggests six lenses or frameworks through which to view the study of play.

The first lens, play as action, depicts play as a pattern of behavior; this is likely the most common viewpoint when studying play. Play is exhibited through physical movements that distinguish it from other forms of behavior. This behavior is individualized, self-directed, and conscious: players are in charge of their actions and determine the meaning of those actions. The play thus leads to personal growth and development. This play perspective leans toward study by the fields of psychology and biology.

The second lens, play as interaction, depicts play as a pattern of behavior with others. Play is not just an isolated endeavor but rather includes something or someone else. In this framework the player engages with the world. This engagement can be with someone or something. The social sciences tend to use this frame as their lens for studying play.

The third lens, play as activity, depicts play in a broader sense of time and space than the previous framework. It typically encompasses named activities, such as racquetball, and as such has broadly defined parameters for participation. The players understand that the type of locale in which play takes place, the behaviors associated with this type of play, and even the amount of time that should be devoted to the activity. This framework leans toward play studies in cultural sciences such as anthropology, folklore, and literature.

The fourth lens, play as disposition, includes the internal or subjective qualities that differentiate play from other forms of behavior or activities. The player exhibits some form of attentiveness, readiness, or commitment to the behavior. In this framework the term *playfulness* means a person's propensity toward finding play possibilities in many situations. This includes curiosity, eagerness, and an openness to play opportunities. This playfulness attitude is a decisive factor in the continuation of play. This aspect of play is heavily studied in the field of psychology.

The fifth lens, play as experience, focuses on the player's awareness and recognition of and satisfaction with what is happening at that specific time. In this perspective, the player is totally absorbed in the moment, much as in the concept of flow that emerged in the work of Csikszentmihalyi (1996). The player is fully absorbed in the experience with a sense of enjoyment in being part of it. Enjoyment is much more open to possibilities, difficulties, and tensions that arise from the experience. This framework is heavily used when sociology and psychology study play.

The sixth lens, play as context, views play in terms of the conditions or particular situations that are influential to the play. For example, many researchers differentiate play from other activities of life by determining whether the activity has minimal adult interference, whether there is an opportunity for free choice, whether the players have had previous experiences playing together, whether the player is familiar with the play objects, and whether or not the player is under stress. These conditions, or contexts, impact the quality of the play. This lens is used by the fields of psychology, education, and recreational studies.

When studying play, it is vital to consider these dimensions and their influence on play. Play provides the context in which a person can discover who they are as an individual and also how they fit within a community or collective perspective. Henricks leaves us with this thought: "If play has a legacy, it is its continuing challenge to people of every age to express themselves openly and considerately in the widest human contexts" (227).

Brian Sutton-Smith, *The Ambiguity of Play*

"We all play occasionally, and we all know what playing feels like. But when it comes to making theoretical statements about what play is, we fall into silliness"

—Brian Sutton-Smith, (1997, p. 1)

Brian Sutton-Smith was one of the foremost play theorists of the late twentieth century. His theoretical works in play were deeply profound and propelled modern play theory into the consciousness of the masses. Sutton-Smith's well-known book *The Ambiguity of Play* created a space for the enormity of this state of being called play.

Sutton-Smith described a list of human behaviors labeled or described as play, but noted that these same activities were often described with other labels, such as entertainment. He arranged his nine play activities from mostly individual to mostly shared activities.

1. **Mind or subjective play** *includes daydreams, fantasy, and imagination.*

2. **Solitary play** *involves such activities as hobbies, collections, or quilting.*

3. **Playful behaviors** *include playing tricks on others or even playing second fiddle.*

4. **Informal social play** *is described as joking or rough-and-tumble play.*

5. **Vicarious audience play** *incorporates parades, concerts, or beauty contests.*

6. **Performance play** *includes such activities as playing a musical instrument or attending theatrical performances.*

7. **Celebrations and activities** *are play activities incorporated into such occasions as birthdays or weddings.*

8. **Contests** *covers such activities as sports and games.*

9. **Risky or deep play** *covers such activities as hang gliding or bungee jumping.*

These categories of play provide a clearer understanding of why it is so difficult to put precise parameters around play. But Sutton-Smith's purpose for the book was not to define or categorize types of play, but rather to provide a framework to better understand the multiple perspectives outlined in play theories. Therefore, he created the seven rhetorics of play and stressed the difference between these rhetorics, whose purpose is to explain or clarify a specific point regarding play versus a narrative about play that simply tells a story. Sutton-Smith's seven rhetorics that relate to self active play are:

1. **Progress:** *play develops knowledge and skills and expresses and builds personal character.*

2. **Self:** *players' experiences are connected to processes or desires, and attaining and being satisfied with what they have attained; play is fun, relaxation, and escape, but it also provides a context in which to sort through range of emotions.*

3. **Imaginary:** *play is an expression of subjectively maintained commitments, an occasion to dream and improvise in processes of construction, presentation, deconstruction, and repair; players create works of art, poetry, and literature.*

4. **Power:** *play involves rivalry, contest, and battle, imposing one's own will on another.*

5. **Identity:** *play connects with community identity; players engage in order to feel their connections with other people and with the customs that guide those interactions.*

6. Fate: *people play to remind themselves that they are not alone in the universe*

7. Frivolity: *play is a form of retrogression or inversion, a retreat into foolishness and insanity.*

The rhetorics of progress, self, and imaginary focus mainly on play scholarship in industrial or "modern" societies. For example, these rhetorics focus on the power of the individual to create or imagine. The rhetorics of power, identity, fate, and frivolity focus on older or more traditional societies, in which there is a fascination with the great forces of the world. The seven rhetorics of play provide a framework for understanding the multiple perspectives associated with play theory and a means by which to compare and contrast each, thus giving each its own voice in the dialogue.

Sutton-Smith used the rhetorics framework in part because each of the seven rhetorics was steeped in a specific discipline of study. For example, the rhetoric of progress permeates in the disciplines of biology, education, and psychology. By anchoring each rhetoric in its specific disciples of study, he promoted validation of the rhetorics as a tool for understanding and creating knowledge about play theories. It should also be noted that Sutton-Smith recognized that talking about play was much different than the actual play experience. From the point of view of the *player* the play experience may very well be a simple passing of time, but from the play theorist's perspective the play event could have significant meaning. For example, a child may be engaged in a simple game of constructing a tower with blocks, but for the play theorist this experience leads to developmental growth in the physical domain by promoting fine motor skills development through the manipulation of the blocks. So, for Sutton-Smith, the ambiguity of play rests firmly in the differences between how play is experienced by the player and how play is studied or perceived by play theorists.

Sutton-Smith concluded "that variability is the key to play, and that structurally play is characterized by quirkiness, redundancy, and flexibility" (Sutton-Smith 1997, 229).

CONCLUSION

THIS CHAPTER REVIEWED what "play" is according to renowned play theorists and researchers. These researchers and theorists have shaped and provided the foundation for developing the meaning, understanding and principles of self active play. As we further explore self active education and play as a medium for learning and development, we must now look at the process and outcomes of play experiences. Self active play is liberating. Players experience a high degree of freedom and inner awakening. From deep within the individual, this form of play mediation causes spontaneous recognition of new knowledge and potential, which portends new positive growth and development within the player. This recognition is an inspiring force revealing the power and promise of self active play.

Chapter 2

Principles of Self Active Play

"Our play is not merely interaction with the external objects, it is interaction with our own sometimes deeply cherished visions. In brief, our play with objects is inevitably self-play"

—Thomas Henricks, p. 82

SELF ACTIVE PLAY is a means of awakening creative potential and providing an opportunity for enjoyable forms of aesthetic self-expression as forms of beauty. The self active play uses open-ended materials in both silent solitary contemplation and cooperative play experiences with both children and adults. This form of play maximizes freedom, self-directed learning, and creative problem solving, all based on our own felt personal interest. Creativity arises during play and stimulates the flow of intuitive insight and self-expression that serves to strengthen resilience and promote healing.

Self active play with adults brings spontaneous recognition of the potential for new growth and more enlightened practice with children. During a professional development workshop, a woman journaled about her solo play.

"To feel so deeply is cathartic, such an intense release. What was I holding on to? What did just happen? It was so visceral, so tactile, so quiet. Just me in my head and heart. Just me being me at the moment being real and vulnerable. Do I not do that often enough? Had I just had it on this sense of everybody trying to impress everyone else? I was making so many connections from my experience from the world around me to what I was touching and doing and seeing. At first, I knew I had to feel the materials under my bare feet and I did. It was all so intuitive and that felt like such a relief for a change. I am always more process-oriented. The mandala I was making with the material fascinated me. I kept changing in my mind what it would be, could be, and should be. Beauty can be found in the impermanence. It flowed and felt right and I let it happen. Then suddenly I destroyed it! This felt like a gift. I found meaning in digging deeper and making connections that came up, connections, and critical thinking. Make the children reflect more in class—they'll have to get better at it."

Playing and making the mandala offers a visual expression of insight, balance, and harmony that symbolizes unity and beauty. The outer form represents the inner wisdom and underlying intuitive principles of self active play that awaken creativity. Play transforms how we learn, what we feel, who we may become, and the way we relate to the world around us.

Seven Principles of Self Active Play

Self active play is based on seven guiding principles, which have grown out of the extensive research and professional work conducted by the Institute for Self Active Education (ISAE). The mission of ISAE is to awaken the creative potential of children and adults through play and art-making. The stories and professional responses shared in this book come from journals, video recordings, and personal interviews generated by the children and adults who have experienced hands-on self active play experiences.

Principle 1:

Play is a source of creative energy, a positive force, and a safe context for constructing meaningful self-knowledge and revitalizing the human spirit across the continuum of the human life cycle.

Principle 2:

Hands-on play and art-making with open-ended materials reconnect the individual with earlier stages of human development, spontaneously balancing and strengthening hope, will, purpose, competence, fidelity, love, care, and wisdom.

Principle 3:

The play space is a state of being that is self-constructed or co-constructed based on the players' previous experiences and their perceptions of the levels of safety and trust leading into the play space.

Principle 4:

Experiences within the play space elicit strong feelings toward the play space, such as protectiveness, a yearning to return, and desire for further exploration of higher levels of understanding and self-awareness.

Principle 5:

The creative energy released within the play space is accelerated as players assume new pretend roles and thrill in discovering "Who will I be next?" and "What will I do next?"

Principle 6:

Play is a source of energy for rekindling love, passion, and intimate relationships with other people and between players. These feelings are pervasive: they are not isolated to the play space but rather move forward as the player moves beyond the play space in their realities.

Principle 7:

Play's intrinsic qualities include spontaneity of the spirit, thinking deeply, feeling intensely, and building trust in one's intuitive self.

These principles lay the foundational beliefs and theoretical framework that inspire creative play leadership and advocacy. Creative energy is within everyone, regardless of age. Energy is released during play encounters as the player discovers new and exciting possibilities. Play is an altered state of being that ignites and rekindles strong feelings within and between those engaged in the play together. Play's inherent qualities promote spontaneity, deep thinking, intense feeling, and the development of confidence in one's intuitive self.

Adults must understand that young children have emotional experiences during their play, just as adults do. However, young children may lack the language capacity to express thoughts and feeling with clarity and complexity. Children and adults alike feel intensely about their play. Play helps us overcome self-doubt and leads us to feel more positive inner power and optimism.

Play itself provides the context for inventing and discovering how to organize and express ideas in aesthetically pleasing and functional three-dimensional visual form. Self active play challenges the senses. Hands, hearts, and minds work together to arrange and construct new compositions that please the player. The doing and the making resonate inward and are felt as competence, surprise, joy. In play there is the freedom to choose and express uniquely in ideas and interests. Play is simply a fundamental healthy human behavior.

Open-ended materials, or loose parts as they are commonly called, of different sizes, shapes, colors, and textures, attract our attention, and engage our senses in a way that stimulates the brain. In the play, we are free to create, engage, and express ourselves with imagination and complexity. As we touch materials, make things, observe, and reflect, we create new possibilities.

"It is a happy talent to know how to play"

—Ralph W. Emerson (as cited in Joel Porte, 1984, p. 138)

Key Outcomes of Self Active Play

1. **Power to Focus:** *Develops the capacity to pay attention, to concentrate.*

   For many children, simply fiddling with objects, stacking one upon the other or laying them end to end, is a deeply satisfying sensory experience. Players focus through their fingertips, concentrating on the task at hand. In this way, they experience the intuitive-self immersed in learning through their capacity to pay attention. Whatever the age, ability level, background, or individual needs of the player, as the player plays with open-ended materials, there is an intentional focus and a dynamic transformation of objects and thoughts into new patterns and relationships. The knowledge derived or constructed from such direct, hands-on personal experience carries with it personal meaning and the power to move to a deeper level of understanding.

2. **Power to Elaborate:** *Develops the capacities of expansion, imagination, vision, and reasoning with complexity and richness of thinking and feeling.*

   Like play with clay and paint and blocks, the nonrepresentational nature of open-ended materials allows players to elaborate on their ideas, to imagine and create, to assign meaning, to define

the purpose, to determine value. This process engenders a feeling of power, self-determination, and authority. Children need to experience these aspects of their lives. Play with open-ended materials helps them to initiate, take charge, and make choices in very simple, safe, and developmentally appropriate ways. This experience helps to form the foundation of competence, an essential and practical skill necessary to live a life with integrity. The self active play process synthesizes content and meaning based on players' direct, concrete manipulative experiences. It helps individuals to make sense of their actions as they play, tinker, and mess about.

3. **Power to Organize Ideas:** *Develops the ability to organize ideas around a central concept, higher ideal, or luminous belief or understanding that will serve as a guide for life.*

   As players build with open-ended materials, they spontaneously connect their ideas and impulses with and through the three-dimensional representations expressed in their play. The interactions between players and the materials are rendered into inner narratives and outer forms or organizing structures that represent elaboration or expansion on ideas that become bigger frameworks or visions that can serve as guides for further development. The act of learning how to put ideas together, of connecting separate yet related elements into a coherent, expressive whole, begins first with materials and then proceeds to abstract symbolic thoughts and ideas that, like objects or materials, relate to one another to form coherent wholeness or a vision. In these relationships, the players form schemata or paradigms for understanding their feelings, thoughts, and assigned value. The abundance and variety of unusual open-ended materials help to inspire and sustain thinking that enables players to elaborate, to create patterns and repeat forms, essentially to create complex systems no one has ever seen before.

4. **Power to Control the Mind:** *Develops the power to inhibit undesirable thoughts so that one may control or regulate what one is thinking about without distraction, sustaining focus on what one wants or chooses to think about when one wants to think it.*

Through the experience of play with open-ended materials and ideas, players gradually develop the capacity to first focus and then begin to elaborate or expand upon the emerging ideas. Players then can further organize and extend their thinking. The extended thinking becomes a general concept or guiding principle, which is made possible by the ability to maintain and control the mind—that is, to engage in positive higher-order thinking or executive function skills.

5. **Power to Quiet the Mind:** *Develops the capacity to silent the mind and calm, peaceful, and thus more receptive to inspirations coming from the heart.*

There is a sense of completeness, balance, peace: a state of "flow." The mind in play is alert open, and relaxed, which is the result of focused, enjoyable, extended, one-pointed mindfulness.

"When teachers play, they learn to see the materials and their possibilities for learning through the eyes of a child."

—Susan Wood, Executive Director,
The Children's Center *California Institute of Technology*

Applying the Principles: Expanding the Conscious Awareness of Play with Adults

In 2017 the authors presented a day of self active play training with teachers and directors of the Jewish Education Project's Conference in New York, *Play is the Way!* Shariee Calderone, Senior Communal Education Consultant shares the following summary of *reflections, learnings, and resources,* which illustrate the power of play to improve the practice of play with children.

"I am more aware of my role as a teacher concerning the way children play! I will go back to the classroom and see if things need to be changed!"

—Workshop participant.

How can early childhood educators skillfully and intentionally guide children's learning through play?

As discourse continues among educators about the loss of play in early childhood and pressure still mounts for educational professionals to present a more "academic" curriculum, we knew it was time to dedicate our annual conference towards a deeper understanding of play and play-based learning. To do this we offered educators time to play to deepen their understanding of the power of play firsthand! Over 400 Jewish early childhood professionals from 60 schools across Westchester, Long Island, Manhattan, and surrounding communities attended one-day workshops. Our conference presenters, Walter F. Drew and Marcia L. Nell, of the Institute for Self Active Education, facilitated the play workshops that incorporated time to play and important reflection time with colleagues. During the workshop, educators were immersed in material-rich play activities. Although it may seem surprising that teachers of two, three, or four-year-old classrooms do not engage in play, the reality is teachers often set up the play for children but rarely experience it for themselves.

"When was the last time you played joyfully?"

This opening question got educators thinking back to their childhood or recent playful moments with their children. Discussions had the participants contemplating the connections between a sense of wonder and play. But it was the intentional play experiences themselves that had the biggest impact on the participants.

Teacher Responses:

Having both solo and cooperative self active play activities back-to-back, with time for reflection and dialogue in between, helped educators understand in a more profound way that each student brings something unique to the play experience and that it all has an effect on others in the group. The participants also noted that in play all children bring with them different interests, personalities, and capabilities. Teacher reflections noted "*During this play, I couldn't stay in the chair. I felt compelled to move around.*" Another teacher commented "*I'm wondering now how children are negotiating with or appeasing other children's tendencies towards controlled orderly play vs more abstract expressive play.*" A third teacher stated, "*I wonder if children feel compelled to use all the materials we put in front of them?*"

Action Plans for Change

An important part of the workshop for educators is putting the learning into context for themselves and their work with children. To do this, participants were asked to journal how the experiences inspired them to take action in their classroom. Here are some examples from those reflections. One teacher journaled, "*Remember the perspective of the child. They are real people with likes and dislikes. Strengths and areas for growth. In attempting to manage a classroom, do not lose sight of this.*" Another teacher noted "*I usually have a plan and a reason as to why I give them certain things to play with. I think it would be great to allow them to use different materials and make things using these random objects. I realized that not everything has to be structured.*" A third teacher expressed that she would, "*Listen carefully to what children say. Learn what they are interested in then provide the prompt/materials. Observe what they do with the materials. Let them discover the joy of learning through play.*" A fourth teacher responded that she would "*Reflect on my expectations for children's play. Do I expect some children to be more interested in group play than they are comfortable with and ready for?*" Finally, one teacher stated, "*I am more aware of my role as a teacher concerning the way children play. I will go back to the classroom and see if things need to be changed!*"

Key Points on "Play Education"

Understanding the process of self active play helps us to understand that play itself is a form of *play education*. As with other types of education, such as science education or math education, "play education" is the practice of teaching and learning about the play. Self active education uses the self active play process as the tool for building and scaffolding one's knowledge and for understanding the richness of play.

In the play reflections shared by Shariee Calderone, we see the power of play to educate. Just like children, teachers constructed meaningful knowledge and made profound discoveries about things that are important to them through play. As teachers, when we play, we create an opportunity for our minds to revel and experience self-discovery and the construction of meaningful knowledge. True education with young children and adults awakens the creative spirit by engaging the hands, heart, and mind in joyful self-discovery and creative expression. There is an inner creative being within everyone, a spirit that seeks to express itself in joyful ways. Self active education offers a safe context in which to discover and celebrate that spirit of play.

Play education offers a process that enriches professional practice. Educating both children and adults about the importance of play is possible and a most worthy goal. Therefore, it is helpful to remember and claim the following assertions to be true and of enormous benefit for adults and children alike.

1. **Play education is an imperative process for helping adults who live and work with children to enhance adult understanding and practice with children.**

   This is true for teachers and parents. Play is the preferred medium of learning for children and a positive force employed in the education of adults. As Peter Gray states, "Everyone, regardless of age, prefers freedom and self-direction to rigid control by others" (2013, 142).

2. **In the self active play, both child and adult feel a sense of control.**

   The players can change the procedures, rules, and modes of expressing their learning and its meaning. Self active play education respects the right of the player to explore and discover. It is the self-activity of the player that enables them to make their discoveries by and about themselves. As Thomas Henricks suggested in his keynote speech at The Association for the Study of Play conference, *The play constitutes a particular pathway of 'self-realization' that distinguishes it from other basic behaviors"* (Henricks 2018).

3. **The adult player must be fully "self active" with open-ended materials, utilizing their full senses— their whole being—if they are to understand the power and wisdom of play.**

This form of education uses play with adults as the cornerstone for real learning. Erik Erikson notes, *"I am persuaded that only by doing and making do we become"* (1997, 127).

4. **Self active play education assumes that the player is interested in the action and therefore willing to participate in the action fully. Children and adults need to be "self-directed."**

   In self-directed play education, players operate on their interests, a keen source of intrinsic motivation. This stimulates creativity and generates a sense of creative purpose. The creative purpose has a positive effect on our mental attitude and disposition, our sense of well-being, and enjoyment of the learning process. As Gray notes, *"The joy of play is the ecstatic feeling of liberty.... play is always accompanied by a feeling of Yes, this is what I want to do right now"* (2013, 141).

5. **Play education satisfies a biological function in the adult as with the child, beginning with the brain's impulse to focus and investigate using all the senses.**

   Given that play is a vital part of the learning process with young children and satisfies a child's natural impulse, it is imperative that adults fully understand this truth through their own direct sensory experience with real open-ended materials. Brown and Vaughn emphasize this point: *"Play seems to be so important to our development and survival that the impulse to play has become a biological drive."* (2009, 42).

6. **Play connects people with themselves and one another, their common interests, and the power to determine how to proceed together.**

   The play spans across the life cycle and therefore significantly affects the future. Froebel notes that "the spontaneous play of the child discloses the future inner life of the man" (2005, 55). Playing well together and having fun are forms of education.

   Based on our research these six considerations are true and constitute a belief system that continues to inspires this work. The simplicity and authenticity of the self active play process have a profound life-long influence on human development.

CONCLUSION

SELF ACTIVE PLAY is a process that can be used with children or adults to develop knowledge and skills. When used with adults, it becomes an educational tool for deeper understanding and transforming professional practice. Self active play is applied research that serves as a readily adaptable process for improving the quality of classroom and professional practice. The self active play process and principles offer a framework for using play as an educational tool.

PART II

PRACTICE OF
SELF ACTIVE PLAY
EDUCATION

Chapter 3

Self Active Play
in Early Childhood Classrooms

*"By education, then, the divine essence of man should
be unfolded, brought out, lifted into consciousness,
and man himself raised into free, conscious obedience
to the divine principle that lives in him, and to a free
representation of this principle in his life."*

—Friedrich Froebel, (2005, p. 4-5)

WHAT HAPPENS FIRST in early childhood influences
what happens later on in adulthood. Self active play provides the opportunity for children to engage in solitary
play as research and investigation. Cooperative play experience offers the additional benefit of collaborative
thinking to the research and investigation. Learning to
enjoy playing both by oneself and with others helps to
ensure greater success and happiness as an adult later on.

Imagine a young child looking up at you after quietly playing
and saying, as he points to a structure he created with open-ended materials, *"This is my space station that sends missiles into the air
and they explode. I made two wings, so if one falls off, there's another
one to save it. I feel happy about making a space station. I learned I
could do it."* That is what a teacher reported following a solitary play

experience with an array of open-ended materials. This child was joyfully present imagining and making and describing his "space station" and what it means to him. In self active play, the child is actively practicing self-regulation as they control the materials and their own actions, paying full attention to what they are doing. This is an example of self-directed play which unifies hands, heart, and mind in a peaceful, inspiring state of creative contemplation. Loris Malaguzzi, (1995, 67), considered the father of the Reggio Emilia approach to education, noted that:

"Children have the right to be recognized as subjects of individual, legal, civil, and social rights; as both source and constructors of their own experience, and thus active participants in the organization of their identities, abilities, and autonomy, through relationships and interaction with their peers, with adults, ideas, things, and with the real and imaginary events of intercommunicating worlds."

Allowing children freedom to imagine and create, strengthens them as citizens of democracy. By encouraging children to develop their inborn abilities, including their creativity, we better equip them to contribute in positive ways to our society. When we fail to honor the rights of the child, they suffer and so does our society.

An early childhood teacher shares her interpretation of a child's silent solo play experience:

"It is a time of contemplation, a meditation. I believe children begin to think and concentrate more when they are quiet and in control. How relaxing it was! The longer the children were involved the more complex their structures and designs became. My very fidgety children also relaxed and concentrated with more attention to what they were building versus distracted bouncing around. They relaxed and became more involved in what they were doing instead of rushing to get done quickly. I was more relaxed and after a while, I began to build as well."

Introducing Silent Solitary Self Active Play in Pre-K

Ellen Grogan is a Pre-K teacher with 26 years of professional practice in Brevard County, Florida. Ellen offers a summary of how she experiments with engaging her four and five-year-old preschool children in solitary self active play:

> *"These Pre-K children need to be active...I plan for 15-20-minute activities. If they like it, they can keep going, if not there are other choices for them. Some kids will be finished before others. There is an option for them. The choice is really important."*

The world of a pre-kindergarten is typically a very busy, noisy place. Since language acquisition in a verbally rich environment is one of the goals of early childhood education, asking 20 four and five-year old children to play quietly by themselves might seem like an unusual and maybe impossible thing to do. Early childhood teachers can help facilitate the play process by providing children with the opportunity and the materials for silent solo play. Ms. Grogan shares:

> *"During the last couple of weeks of school, while doing our work time part of the day, I introduced my children to Dr. Drew's Discovery Blocks, little purple foam cylinders, and red and yellow plastic caps of varying sizes. I asked the children to play quietly for a little while by themselves. The children were positioned around the room on the floor and at tables so that they each had space to play and create. I gave each child an ample supply of the building materials and encouraged them to explore and create whatever they wanted to with their supplies. And then the building began!"*

The teacher has an important role to assume as the children are engaged in silent solo play. The teacher scaffolds the children's play experience by providing "quiet" reminders and making careful observations.

"I walked around the room, encouraging the quiet. If some-one started talking or was off task, I gently redirected their attention. In general, it was a quiet, busy hive of activity. Several children started building fairly elaborate vertical structures while others made more simple linear horizon-tal structures. Some knocked theirs down and then started again, while others continued building and adding to the original structure. The foam pieces and colorful caps were not only used to decorate their structures but also to rep-resent a variety of items or parts of structures, such as a space station, a throne, cupcakes, lasers for security, rocket launchers, and walkways."

In thinking about science or STEM related content and the process of visualizing, investigating, designing and engineering ways of putting things together and representing an idea, structure or phenomenon, self active play offers a perfect context. Giving an interesting abundance of open-ended materials inspires them to imagine, connect and describe their expressions in three-dimensional form.

"After about 20 minutes, I took time to go around the room and visit with each of these young architects, engineers and builders to ask them if there was something they would like to share about the experience. Some of the children offered very detailed explanations and others made simple com-ments about their creation."

One of the many amazing phenomena that can occur during silent solo play is the ingenuity and resourcefulness that children display. Ms., Grogan notes:

"One particular structure of interest was a large sprawling creation that had a centerpiece and then other areas con-nected by block walkways. The piece in itself was interest-ing, but during the twenty minutes that I observed the chil-dren constructing, two of the children, a boy, and a girl had

joined their pieces and were working together. I hadn't heard any verbal agreement to this, they just did it. I had watched and videotaped them building in the block area about four months ago. During that work time, they were trying to figure out how to build a roof on their structure, and had given each other ideas, told each other if they thought something would work, and had worked side by side for over forty minutes. Seeing that process happen during our quiet work time without verbal communication was fascinating."

Silent solo play is an experience that opens pathways for a child to explore the depths of possibilities that pop up in their own minds as they play. It provides the child with a context for solving problems and fixing dilemmas. Ms. Grogan observes:

"There are several factors to take into consideration about this activity. First of all, with a couple of exceptions, the students have been together all year, interacting in a variety of settings with each other all day, every day. Secondly, the developmental level of the students varies greatly, as is frequently observed in their interactions and their play. Seeing a simple structure built and then torn down, right next to an elaborate structure that continued to be embellished, was not unusual. Play like this typically proceeds without comments about the other structures. The students seem to take in stride that varying degrees of difficulty in the building process is no big deal. Also, while this activity was new to the students, throughout the school year I have introduced many different and varied activities, so the children were comfortable with this novel process."

In this busy, hectic and often troubled world of ours, where our classrooms, homes, cars, environment, and devices provide so much stimulation to internalize, it seems like teaching children how to calm down and quiet their minds is a worthy goal. Quiet solitary self active play is a contemplative experience, a time for them to think by themselves, to sit quietly and ponder, plan, initiate, create, follow-through, describe and share.

"Aside from seeing the children build and create, watching them work in quiet was very interesting. As I mentioned ear-lier, our classrooms are rich in language, and language is typically heard, spoken, and thus has some element of noise attached to it. We encourage the use of "words" throughout our day to let us know what they are thinking, to let others know what we need, or to be able to simply express them-selves. During our school day, we teach a variety of simple, and sometimes strange things. We teach letters and what sound they make, shapes, numbers, counting, colors, days of the week, how to line up, how to wash hands, to flush, cough into your elbow, use a tissue instead of a finger, how to fold a blanket, how to say I'm sorry, how to clean-up, and too many more to mention. After seeing how much the children enjoyed quiet solitary play, it seems to me that facilitating an opportunity for them to practice the process involved should be added to our list of things to do."

We see in Ms. Grogan's story how one teacher finds a way to engage her children in quiet solitary play. Children are encouraged to play quietly by themselves using open-ended materials. There is soft instrumental music playing in the background. The teacher prepares the environment and supports the children's play by being present and available, but not intrusive. The teacher steps back, yet listening, observing, and documenting the children's play. This is an essential consideration.

In just a few moments of quiet solitary play, children focus and self-regulate. Children discover ways of making things happen as they arrange objects, imagine, and create narratives to their play stories. When children or adults engage in self active play, they practice exercising initiative, making choices, creating, and think-ing with imagination which unlocks insight, healing, and joy.

Steps to Engaging Children in Silent Solitary Self Active Play in the Classroom

1. Invite the children to play with a set of open-ended materials.

Ask the children to play quietly by themselves for just a little while. Ask the children to please not talk during this quiet play time. Allow the time and freedom for the children to explore and use the materials as they wish. This is a time for the teacher to remain present and observe what the children are doing. Teachers should avoid the temptation to seize upon the teachable moment by asking a question, making a suggestion, or otherwise influence the children's thinking while they are focused and engaged in their play. This is a natural inclination of teaching, but this is a time for the teacher to remain silent. Questions and suggestions come after the children have had the opportunity to explore and create with autonomy. Teachers remain ready to make notes of their thoughts and feelings as they observe the children engage in the process of open-ended exploration and discovery. This type of self active play may last for five to ten, or twenty minutes or more, depending on the children's age or experience and the ambiance of the learning environment. The teacher is cognizant of the children's capacity for focused attention and elaboration. The goal is to provide the play opportunities for children to develop and strengthen their capacity for concentration and more elaborate thinking and creative problem solving.

"Throughout the daily hustle and bustle in the classroom, I have found that dimming the lights and giving the children some quiet playtime has had a positive impact on the class as an entirety. The children calm themselves down and will either engage with a peer or independently during the quiet playtime. During this time, I will either place a variety of manipulatives on carpet squares and/or at the tables, enough for each child to have something to engage with. Over time and with more exposure to quiet play the children are eventually able to independently choose what they want to use during quiet playtime. First is exposure, followed with the practice of quiet play kept within their weekly routine, and then observing and documenting the success and benefits of quiet play."

—Early Childhood Educator, Danbury, CT

Here is an example of how another teacher introduced the solitary play to her whole group of children:

"Boys and girls, I have something very special to share with you today. You can see there are some materials placed on fabric pieces all around the room. Let's take a few minutes and look over the materials. Please take a walk around the room to look at or touch the materials.

"Now that you've looked over the materials, sit down next to a set of materials that you are curious about. For the next few minutes, we are going to play quietly with these materials. I'll put on some quiet music and while you are playing, I will walk around the room and observe what you are doing and making.

"Please stay with the set of materials you chose for the whole time. Remember to play quietly by yourself for a few minutes without talking to anyone else. There will be time for all of us to talk after we've had a chance to play. I will let you know a couple of minutes before it is time to stop playing. Then we will take some time for you to share the story about what happened during your play."

2. **Observe the children as they play, walk around the room observing, quietly, documenting, and photographing what you see as the children play.**

Be an active observer and listener. This is a time for you to make notes about what the children are doing as they play. Use digital cameras, iPods, and cell phones as a tool for documenting what the children are doing with the materials. As mentioned in the earlier chapter, it is useful to get in the habit of taking photos of the children's play that illustrates the progress of their construction. This alleviates any child being left out and it provides evidence of the child's play from a chronological lens. This is the time to collect evidence and pay attention to the child's activities. Children are aware that the teacher's time is important. The children observe that the teacher is using that time to observe and be present with them during their play. Typically, there is nothing the teacher must say as the children play.

Since this may be a new experience for some children, they may need additional support in their development of self-regulation. Occasionally, it is necessary to help these children. Here is an example from one teacher of how she scaffolded the children's self-regulation:

"My children are exposed to self-soothing, regulation, cognitive, fine motor, math, literacy, and social-emotional skills during our quiet playtime. I have found that the children had a hard time calming down the first couple of times I introduced quiet play. However, throughout the year the children gained an understanding and an eagerness to have quiet play often.

"It can be difficult at first because the children are not customarily introduced to the concept of quiet play. This is why I try to start at the beginning of the year and continue weekly with it."

—*Early Childhood Teacher*

3. **Give a warning when the play is about to end.**

If children are immersed and wish to continue exploring beyond the allotted time, if at all possible, let them do so. Here is an example of how one teacher gave the 2-minute warning to her whole group of children:

"Boys and girls, in a minute or so we will have a chance to talk about our play."

4. Ask the children to pause in their play, sit quietly for one moment, close their eyes, relax, breathe deeply, slowly inhaling and exhaling.

This moment of sitting quietly is a mindfulness practice, that allows the child to focus and be more aware of their actions and what just occurred in their play. Keep time as the children reflect for one minute. Here is an example of how one teacher invited the children to reflect:

"OK, boys and girls, it's time for us to stop playing and to find out what happened during the play. Please sit quietly for one minute. Close your eyes, relax, take a deep breath, and let it out slowly. I'm looking at my watch and I will let you know when one minute is up."

5. Ask the children to reflect on their play experience.

This can be done through drawing and/or writing to represent what they did with the materials in some way that pleases them. Encourage the children to simply describe what they did during their play, what they made, or how they feel. This opportunity helps children make the connection between the physical experience of arranging materials and the symbolic expression of that experience. It is a form of storytelling that emerges naturally from the play experience. Here is an example of how one teacher invited the children to express their play:

"Boys and girls, please take a few minutes to draw a picture or write about what you did in your play. What did you see? What happened? How did you feel? Put your ideas on the paper."

6. Invite the children to "buddy-up" with a friend and take turns telling about their play experience.

This enjoyable activity develops listening skills and the ability to share and describe the experience. This process may take 3-5 minutes for each of the children to tell their stories about their play. Explain that only one person speaks while the other person listens. They take turns sharing. This way of sharing works best if the children realize that they each have an uninterrupted opportunity to express their thoughts and feelings. They hear themselves think out loud and relate the content of the play experience spontaneously. Also, taking turns sharing frees the listener to be one-pointed in listening rather than talking. Here is one possible way of instructing the children to share their play with another:

"Boys and girls, please find a partner. You each take turns sharing what you did during your play. First, one of you will be the speaker while the other person will be the listener. Listen carefully to your partner speaking without saying anything. Be present and just listen until it is your turn to talk."

7. Invite the children to take a turn and share their play experience with the whole group.

Suggest that there is a little story in everyone's play experience. Ask them to describe what they did, what happened, and how it felt to them. This is a time for you to share your observations about the children, noting highlights and successes you observed. Encourage the children to realize the power of play and the different ways that people express themselves. Acknowledge their ability to create harmony and order. Here is a question that will inspire conversation when sharing the play with the whole group:

"Boys and girls, is there anything you would like to share about your play experience with the whole group?"

Some prompting or follow-up comments or questions can draw out more information from the children. The teacher's response needs to relate directly to the children's narrative and to what you observed the children doing. For instance, observing one child in play you noticed their careful use of STEM-related skills and shared your observation, such as:

"I see you balanced the blocks carefully. Can you tell me what you did to make the structure so strong?"

8. Lead the children on a Walk About/ Talk About.

Talk a walk around the classroom together, stopping at each of the children's work so everyone can see and discuss all the various creations made by all of the children in the classroom. This part of the reflective process provides opportunity for all of the children to ask questions and share ideas. This is a very important part of group development, creating a sense of community within a classroom setting. This may not be an easy process to establish with twenty young children and time constraints, but it is something to strive for within a classroom, perhaps in small steps. Try it and see where adjustments must be made for your classroom as you adjust to the experience. This whole process demonstrates active research.

Here is an example of how one teacher invited the children to participate in the Walk About/Talk About:

"Let's take a walk around the room and see what everybody did during their play. Let's go right along here and walk together to Sally's play and see what she has to say. After she's finished, if we have some time left, we can ask her some questions or share our responses."

9. Lead a group summary discussion about the children's play experiences.

This process includes a summary of ideas and interests, concepts, and skills expressed or revealed in their play. To get started, ask the children questions to help make them aware of their interests, their friends' interests, and where they may like to take their play next. From the response of the children, we learn their interests, level of understanding, and what they have learned through play. Here is an example of how one teacher invited the children to summarize their play:

"Boys and girls, what did you learn from your experience today? What did you enjoy about the play? What follow-up activity might you like to do?"

Children enjoy their reflection and group discussion and learn about one another. Listen carefully to the children to see if there is something you can do to extend their learning. In essence, this is building the curriculum on the interests of the children with the thoughtful, professional guidance of the teacher. When the teacher provides time and opportunity for children to play and reflect, they help children to understand the meaning and relevance it holds for them. The reflective summary process is a good way to help children understand how they're learning and what else they may want to explore and know about. It is a way of helping children synthesize their learning that nurtures a relationship with one's self and with others.

As other children share and listen to their friends talk about their play experience, they may be interested in the same kind of things and want to collaborate or play together. This is one-way relationships are constructed and strengthened. As a way of documenting and validating the children's responses, record or write down on large poster paper what the children say about their play during group discussion. You can then use the chart as a reference point for assessing next steps or follow-up content areas and activities that will help children reconnect and advance their learnings.

Steps to Engaging Children in Cooperative Self Active Play in the Classroom

Another type of self active play is called cooperative play, and it is an essential part of Developmentally Appropriate Practice in early education, especially when it comes to social-emotional development. Quiet solitary play helps to set the stage for the more robust cooperative play. We encourage you to do the quiet solitary play experience first. Cooperative play, by contrast to solitary play, encourages creative, cooperative interaction with other children, a valuable way for developing social and emotional skills. For those children who struggle with initiating an activity, cooperative play with a partner can help. There may be some children who have a difficult time knowing what to do or how to begin to play cooperatively with other children. Play with a partner helps children overcome resistance, lack of interest, and self-doubt about their abilities. In the company of another child who hasn't developed adequate cooperative skills, the partner play can help stimulate a way of moving forward. An early childhood teacher notes:

"During cooperative play, I would advise teachers to avoid providing feedback for the children while they are engaged in play. The children are more inclined to become distracted when this happens. I also advise teachers to provide their students with an abundance of materials to use so that the children have multiple avenues to express their creativity and are not limited by a lack of resources. The children should decide which materials are best suited for their purpose and then provide them with opportunities to utilize them in a meaningful way that maintains their interest."

Cooperative play helps children to scaffold their own learning in the company of others. Learning to negotiate, compromise, co-operate and solve problems together are supported safely using the self active play protocols. Risk-taking is a natural part of coopera-tive play as children work together and encourage one another to express their ideas. Comments concerning compromise are often heard as children play, listen, construct and adapt in order to ac-complish their collaborative mission. One early childhood teacher reflects about her experience using self active play in her classroom:

"The challenges of social dynamics was a little exhausting, but I became more convinced that balancing solitary and cooperative play is key. Some children need that time to play by themselves in order to become a better cooperative player. As a facilitator of play, I think understanding the role of the teacher in cooperative play is a tricky one for most teach-ers. Many teachers want to jump right into the children's play to help them problem solve and handle conflicts. They may also want to lead the play in a different direction. I am convinced that making observations and noticing coopera-tive play behaviors can give teachers many missing pieces to understanding the children. Lots of play time is needed for children to develop social and emotional skills - who takes the lead, who offers new ideas, who cooperates."

Here are some practical suggestions for practicing cooperative self active play with children.

1. Invite the children to share materials as they explore and create together.

In the beginning, you may want to set the number of young children to be in the group. The smaller the number, the easier for the children to get along. You may also decide who you want to work together may also be something to consider for the teacher. Here is an example of how one teacher invited the children to participate in cooperative play:

"You'll remember the fun we had using the materials in solitary play. This time, the idea is for you to use the materials in your group to make something that you all feel good about. You begin by talking about what to do or by touching the materials and seeing what happens next. Do something together and see what happens. Just like you did in solitary play, I'll keep time and let you know when we get near the end of today's activity. We'll take some time to share what happened. Playing together is a very special gift. We don't want to forget how wonderful it is to have a friend and doing things together, sharing ideas and materials, asking questions, solving problems, finding ways of building things together. Play is a very special way to learn how to do that."

2. Stay nearby and present with the children as they play.

Walk around the room listening, observing quietly, and documenting what you see as the children play. Be an active observer and an active listener. Just like in the solitary play experience, the teacher's presence is important. In the cooperative play, there may be opportunities for the teacher to join the conversation or thoughtfully offer a guiding provocation. There are also opportunities to suggest or add props to enrich and extend the children's play. It is best to pause and reflect before entering the children's play. The teacher observes the children's learning and perhaps makes helpful suggestions directly related to the concerns or problems the children are exploring, then moves out of the play. An early childhood play coach/trainer observed and responded to the children's play:

"I was wondering if this would be helpful to you. Would this block help with your building? Did you see those foam pieces over there? I overheard you talking about a river. Could you use this piece of blue fabric?"

3. Give the children a two-minute warning.

As in other activities, children benefit from having a warning before it's time to stop. The advance warning is a way to ease the transition that is about to happen. This provides the children with the opportunity to finish up and make a smoother transition. Here is an example of how one teacher gives the two-minute warning:

"Boys and girls, in a minute or so, if you are ready, we will have a chance to talk about our cooperative play."

4. Allow time for reflecting within the small groups.

Each member should have an opportunity to share thoughts and feelings, all of which are accepted as a valid part of personal experience. Here is an example of how one teacher opened the group reflection about the cooperative play:

"Boys and girls, please take a few minutes in your small groups to share what happened, what you think is important and tell your friends. Did you like the experience? Did you learn anything new? I'll give you a minute warning before we transition."

5. Lead the Walk-About, Talk-About.

Model how to listen, be sensitive, and respond thoughtfully with each group member. Allow everyone to talk about the experience from his or her perspective—what each child did, how it felt, what everyone learned, what insights or difficulties arose, what ideas or suggestions came up for discussion? Here is an example of how one teacher encouraged Walk About/Talk About:

"Boys and girls, as we move around the room we'd like to hear from at least one person from each group. Share with us what your group did, what your group discovered."

The teacher recognizes opportunities to support the children's interests and development. Encourage sharing in the full group so players can discuss what they learned and what they may like to do next. Pose questions to explore differences between solitary and cooperative play, the qualities of team behavior, and individual preferences that happened during play. Note that insights gained through sharing and contrasting differences between solitary and cooperative play reveal personal preferences and more effective play together.

6. Lead a group summary of the cooperative play experience.

Allow children to summarize or tell their cooperative play "story". This helps to extend and deepen children's thinking and understanding of what they just experienced during play. The teacher may need to provide more support as the children may initially find it difficult to summarize their thoughts about the play. The teacher responds by recognizing and sharing what she heard the children say as she gathers hints of ideas and interests expressed by the children. This is an opportune moment to offer suggestions to extend their new learning.

"When children talk with one another it is easier to identify their curiosities and knowledge. It was not until the end of the activity, during their reflections, that I discovered what they were building. What is even more interesting is how the children worked together cooperatively without knowing the intentions and planning of their peers. Being present with the children while they participated in quiet play allowed me to step back into a more observational role and truly notice and document what the children were doing. I was able to see how resourceful the children were on their own, without instruction and preconceived ideas or suggestions from me. The children became their own experts in learning and maintaining their autonomy throughout their play experience. I was able to appreciate and respect each child's thought process and allow the environment and the child to take part in the self-teaching process."

—Paola Lopez, Founder & Director,
Kinderoo Children's Center, Ocala, FL

Dealing with Constraints of Time, Space, and Materials

"I often have a time restraint of 20 minutes and offer children the choice of playing by themselves or joining with friends after the first 5 minutes of exploring the materials. My kids loved to play at their innovation stations!! We used the following materials throughout the year: flat marbles, cardboard, foam cubes, tissue paper, straws, plastic insulin tops, yarn, wooden blocks, and foam shapes. When first starting I had my students work independently in a quiet space on the carpet and then when they showed that they could "earn" working with partners by taking care of the materials, they got to choose whether they wanted to work with their partners (2-4 kids at a time) or wanted to work independently. My students would build animals, make up their games, and pretend to be engineers building castles and bridges. Every single student looked forward to innovation stations and they were sad if we ran out of time and their group didn't make it there for the day. I observed that some of my students struggled to share and listen to other ideas grow tremendously. They worked together because they were having fun and knew their partners could help them in constructing their ideas when they struggled to do so independently. Also, I loved watching my student problem-solve with a smile on their face instead of tears running down their face when they were faced with a challenge in their design. Thank you so much for teaching us and reminding us all how important having fun is and all the lessons that can be taught while doing."

—KIPP School First Grade Teacher

Perhaps you feel that you don't have time to do both solitary or cooperative play on the same day. As children arrive, they know to move to the area with the materials and begin their day with quiet play. You may have quiet music playing in the background. This provides children the opportunity to collect their thoughts, calm their emotions, and be ready for the school day to begin.

Self active play is driven by several key factors. The disposition of the teacher is a highly influential factor. It helps if the teacher has patients and willingness to explore and experiment with the children. Other critical concerns are the *amount of time available, the number of children playing, materials available, and the interest and developmental level of the children.* If time, space or materials are a challenge, begin by thinking of a quiet place for just one child to play with materials. This would be a modest way to begin the process. An option would be a space to accommodate two children playing together on the floor and table with open-ended materials.

Setting up a large table for children to engage in play as they arrive at the beginning of the day is another option that supports focus and informal discussion prompted by sharing materials and ideas. Just doing that would be fantastic. An adequate supply of high-quality open-ended materials works best for self active play. These are unusual reusable resources that have no defined purpose. Choose materials that spark curiosity, imagination, and are likely to sustain engagement and promote rich, elaborate thinking children.

Materials: A Positive Business Perspective

Local businesses are willing to be part of a professional support system that provides unique and exciting instructional materials for teachers, children, parents, and artists to reuse as tools for hands-on creative learning. Art Hoelke and Valerie Ryan are leaders of two companies that have been contributing a variety of discarded materials from their manufacturing processes to the Reusable Resource Adventure Center for more than a decade. Art Hoelke, is General Manager and Vice President of Knight's Armament Company in Titusville, Florida.

"My entire motivation for donating our discard materials has been to touch the lives of young children and teachers. I look at donating our unwanted foam and wooden sticks as a very easy way for business and industry to help students build skills and achieve success through more hands-on learning. We're talking about clean, safe items that our company normally sends to the landfill as excess by-products. I see this process as a viable way to build our future workforce and give our children the best possible way to succeed. We are working together as a community to help promote quality education. This helps our community to grow!

"We as a business community must work together and be more involved in making things better for our children and youth. There are 500 manufacturers in our community. Imagine the resources we are wasting which can be redirected to promote higher order thinking and team-work for improving outcomes for the future of our students."

(Hoelke 2018)

Valerie Ryan, is the Principal Research Scientist at MRI Global Bio-surveillance Division in Palm Bay, Florida. Dr. Ryan is involved with programs in the areas of national security and defense, life sciences, energy and the environment, agriculture and food safety, and engineering and infrastructure.

"In our work as applied scientists, creative thinking and problem solving are important skill sets. Hands on exploration during method development is a big part of what we do as scientists. Finding a unique solution to a problem is brought about by imagination, brainstorming the ideas, visualizing and testing the approach and validation of the method through further testing; but it all starts with the ability to think creatively.

"After seeing the value of our cast off items as inspiration for hands-on learning and creative thinking in children and teachers, we began donating unwanted materials to our local reuse center. I envision developing a larger depot to receive, store, sort and offer materials to teachers and the community. Establishing a network of centers across the state would help to make materials available to many more teachers and children. Getting the message out to other businesses could help springboard the vision. Businesses may provide further support through philanthropic funding, and increased streams of unique and interesting items to supply the network of centers."

Materials: Resources for Awakening Creativity

Materials are tools for awakening creativity and empowering self discovery. Sue Blandford is the Founding Director of the St. Louis Teachers Recycle Center and a Master Play Coach. Sue shares how play with simple materials awakens imagination and creative thinking.

"A pile of grandma's buttons, her shoe box of old thread spools or driftwood and seashells collected from a beach once walked reconnect me with the places and people I cherish. Bits of found materials draw me in because of my preference for color, texture and form. Exploring and discovering their properties is a reflective journey in research, 'At first I just sorted everything and then my mind went quiet and my hands took over'. 'What will happen if I place this here?' 'This did not stack the way I want.' 'I kept trying and trying'. Organizing and sorting become decisions I make when I begin my play. Making order out of chaos I gain a sense of control. My ideas, hopes, dreams and fears come from my life experiences and get played out in front of

my eyes. Tumbling together with feelings, this new experience transforms my understanding and beliefs without prescribed outcomes. I am free to design and be the creator of new knowledge. My new perspective on the world becomes a powerful motivation to learn more. The play with materials becomes a language to share what I know and a journey to discover more. Materials become the provocation, beckoning me to explore and awaken creativity and new possibilities with children and adults."

How Materials Transform Professional Practice

Paola Lopez Founder, Executive Director Kinderoo Children's Academy (Preschool) shares how her teachers transformed classroom practice when materials were available.

"What we once saw as garbage, we now see as creative resources with endless possibilities. That's what happened after a hands-on professional development workshop! Our teachers now use open-ended recyclable materials in every corner of their classroom. We have incorporated more blocks, created an art studio, and an engineering/makers room that's filled with materials that have been recycled by our families and the Reusable Resources Adventure Center in Melbourne, Florida. Slowly, we are learning to make our own learning resources which in many cases are free and more enjoyable for the children.

"We have learned to present the materials in an attractive way that stimulates curiosity and encourages the children to play, build and create art. We now view and respect the children as young artists, builders, and investigators of their own world. It is amazing to observe children playing and using their creativity to manipulate materials in new and unconventional ways.

"In the past I preferred to buy and use store bought toys, but I did not know that giving children open ended recyclable materials, gives children more opportunities to develop their creative and analytical thinking skills, vocabulary, math and even social emotional skills".

Observing Cooperative Play Emerge in the Classroom

Observing Sophia and Ryan, two four-year-old children engaged in self active play, we witness their imaginative storytelling, cooperation, and creativity emerge as they play together. The teacher placed empty spools of thread and giant-size craft sticks on an outdoor table. Sophia looked at them for a moment and then began to stack the craft sticks on the empty wooden spools.

Spontaneously, she began to build her fish tank. Two leaves found on the ground were added to represent fish. Sophia was very proud and protective of her creation. Her friend Ryan came over to see what Sophia was doing. Ryan was very impressed with Sophia's fish tank and decided to build her own. Sophia had no problem sharing the materials, but she wanted Ryan to build her own structure while she continued to work on her fish tank alone. Sophia added details to her fish tank by creating a cover so that "the people could look up through a window to see the fish."

Ryan created a fish tank similar to Sophia's then decided it was a shark tank. Ryan said she was "building a tank and putting five sharks in the tank, noting that she needed to cover the tank so the sharks couldn't bite people. Ryan used five leaves for the sharks. Sophia then added more fish to her tank. When Ryan suggested they connect their tanks, Sophia refused because sometimes her fish get scared.

The teacher realized that Sophia had valid reasons for not wanting to mix her fish with sharks. After finishing their fish tanks, the girls began to work on a third tank together. They continued to build together, and at one point, Ryan gathered all the craft sticks and placed them in front of her. Sophia was upset that Ryan took all of the craft sticks. Ryan then gave Sophia more craft sticks after Sophia complained. Ryan suggested to Sophia that they build a ramp across the top of the two fish tanks. Sophia agreed. Sophia then ran out of materials but was not finished with the aquarium.

The teacher suggested that the girls look on the manipulatives shelf to see if anything would work for the aquariums. Sophia found building materials on the shelf and brought the new materials over for Ryan and her to use. The girls began to stack the "connecting blocks" on top of their aquarium. At first, the girls were stacking the connecting blocks individually, but as the tower became higher, the task became more difficult. The girls then began to help each other. One would hold the structure while the other connected the next piece. At one point the structure collapsed and Ryan was upset. The teacher suggested they repair the structure by putting the wooden spools under the craft sticks. Ryan followed the teacher's suggestion, and it worked. After Ryan made repairs they decided their aquariums were complete.

Sophia spent thirty minutes on her aquarium, and Ryan spent twenty-four minutes on hers. The teacher was impressed by the amount of time the girls spent working on their structures and how organized they were. The girls worked well together, using valuable social skills to solve problems. They also used trial and error to build the structure, especially after the structure collapsed. They learned as they balanced the connecting blocks on top of the original structure, that they must have proper support so the structure would hold the weight. The girls' interactions and verbal planning helped the structure become more detailed. The girls gained confidence as they faced new challenges. The teacher acknowledged and praised the girls, not only on their cool structures but also on their sharing and using kind words as they played together. Photos were taken of the completed project and hung in the classroom. Each girl got a photograph to keep so that they could share their creation with parents.

As with Ryan and Sophia, during self active play, all children are learning to self-regulate their own emotional responses in order to achieve a common goal. This is an essential human ability needed to survive happily in the world as an adult. In presenting self active play experiences with young children or adults, how we interact with others—how we present our views, our power, our state of mind—automatically exerts an influence on the children and adults around us. Learning to be mindful of how our power and influence impacts others is a critical awareness that children begin to learn in rich early childhood play experiences. How we use our power is important when working with children or adults. The authors share the point of view that all children who are skilled at playing with both things and ideas will have more power, influence, understanding, and capacity to create meaningful lives for themselves as adults. Children who are skilled at finding order and inspiration when faced with ambiguity and uncertainty are better prepared to create solutions to problems that are at first overwhelming. In play, children learn strategies, skills, and attitudes needed to overcome and solve real life problems.

Professor's Reflection of
Self Active Play Experience

Sean Durham, a professor at Auburn University, shares his experience of a professional development play workshop at the National Association for the Education of Young Children (NAEYC) Annual Conference. Here are his thoughts as he reflects on this adult play experience:

"The play experience in which I participated allowed me to witness dedicated professionals who are serious about the value of play in the lives of young children and recognize that adult play provides a pathway toward enlightenment. Specific instructions were given in the first play experience. For example, 'clear the table of your stuff', represents what most adults need to do in order to enter into play themselves and to truly appreciate the play of children. 'Play silently by yourself' was offered as instruction for the solitary play experience. It is difficult to suspend the active mind that is filled with thoughts and emotions about our daily realities. I found that the silent play experience opened my mind to see myself as a creative force as I interacted with the simple materials. 'See where you and the objects go' encouraged me to approach the materials and the play experience with openness. I remembered looking at my hands and some materials that were close by. I didn't have any idea what I wanted to do, so I just picked up a simple block and placed it on its end. Soon, there was a gathering of blocks in proximity to one another, which served as a foundation.

"From that experience I realized what Dr. Drew means when he encouraged us to 'let one action lead into the next, to go with the flow'. This simple act of placing the blocks created a flow of energy that produced a series of thoughts and actions. 'Content will arise within you that you cannot

now anticipate' was very interesting to me. This is one of the most astounding things that I have learned through the play workshops. On a physical level, the arrangements of materials and the subsequent structure emerged in a way that I had not predicted or planned. Play truly is a creative force. When play happens, forces of creativity flow through the brain and body. This flow and our reflection upon what was created through play, reinforces our concepts of ourselves as creative beings."

CONCLUSION

IT'S DIFFICULT TO fully appreciate the extraordinary value of self active play for children without having a personal experience with the process. Solitary and cooperative self active play are grand adventures for children, as well as adults. And a grand adventure especially for the teacher! This process enables the teacher to "let go" and give children control of their learning without knowing the outcome before it happens. Giving children the freedom to take the lead and direct their learning through play helps to assure positive outcomes for both children and teachers. That is, in part, what makes this a grand adventure. The teacher is free to explore and discover with the children. Together the adventure of self active play fulfills the goal of being a professional early childhood educator.

Loris Malaguzzi (1995, 67) agrees that the rights of children are recognized when they are given the opportunity to play freely. Play is the context for children to learn social skills, how to care and trust one another. While at the same time, children are expressing a developmental need to be creative that all children have. The purpose of the relationship between the adult and the child is to foster the child's creation of thought and action. This critical alliance between the child and the adult is the heart of teaching.

Chapter 4

Putting It All Together:
Improving Professional Development
and Classroom Practice

*"Play is one of the unseen, unsung marvels of the universe,
a ceaseless creator whose rules are governed by the many
and varied laws of harmony."*

—Kate Ransohoff, (2006, p. 29)

PROFESSIONALS ARE EXPECTED to learn and grow predominantly with verbal instruction only, and yet the principles of self active play can easily contribute to a more effective course of study. Our story begins in firm support of the statement by Jean Piaget, "The goal of education is not to increase the amount of knowledge but to create the possibilities for a child to invent and discover, to create men [and women] who are capable of doing new things" (Whitman, A. 1980, p. 4). This challenging educational goal is fundamental to the process called self active education. During self active play, children actively construct knowledge about open-ended objects, developmental processes, problem-solving strategies and create images of themselves as competent and emotionally healthy learners. Through physical interaction with the environment, children come to realize their power to exert influence in the world.

In this chapter, we will examine self active play as a professional development method that transforms teachers' professional practice. In Manatee County, Florida, forty-one preschool teachers implemented a new, inquiry-based curriculum consisting of four science-based units. In one of these units, early childhood teachers and early learning specialists from the district engaged in constructive play using Dr. Drew's Discovery Blocks and other open-ended materials in support of the Buildings and Structures unit (Nell & Drew, 2013).

Effective Professional Development

It is well known that teacher quality makes a difference in student achievement (Goldhaber, 2016). Over the last fifty years, educational researchers digging into the variables that impact student learning continue to show that teachers make a difference. Another interesting finding indicates that over 75 percent of veteran teachers rely on professional development as their main avenue for staying up to date, in tune with current practices, and developing new knowledge in their fields (Jaquith, Mindich, Wei, & Darling-Hammond 2010). Knowing these two major facts, it is vitally important to provide early childhood teachers with the best and most valuable professional development, so they are able to construct and then translate newly formed knowledge into professional practices that engage our young children in the highest quality experiences.

Current research on professional development has determined that several components need to be present in order for professional development to manifest change in professional practices. According to Han (2014), professional development needs to provide teachers with guidance to reflect on their own practices. Bayar (2014) indicated that effective professional development must include active participation, engagement over time, and highly skilled and knowledgeable instructors. Jaquith et. al (2010) found that effective professional development must be focused on a specific component of the curriculum. Teachers need to be highly engaged to make sense of and try out the idea. Professional development must be intensive, sustained, and continuous to make changes in teacher practices. It must be linked to teaching and learning and also supported by coaching and modeling. The self active play process used as a tool for professional improvement meets all of these requirements for successful professional development. The self active play experience encourages transformation of professional practice.

Stage 1, the encounter, prepares players for active participation in a hands-on play experience with open-ended materials. The participants are highly engaged and focused on their play, with sustained, intensive concentration.

Stage 2, the reflective process, is when participants are carefully guided through a series of practices that tie their experience to both their teaching practice and what children experience while in a deep state of self active play.

Stage 3, the synthesis, enables participants to make connections between their play experience, how children experience play, and how these experiences shape perspectives on learning and teaching. Thus, the self active play experience is an effective tool for professional development that promotes personal growth, deep understanding of play, and effective professional practices to support children's learning and development.

According to Jeffrey and Craft, "teachers who work creatively employ both *creative teaching* and *teaching for creativity* according to circumstances they consider appropriate" (as cited in Craft 2005, 44). The researchers suggest that teachers who model creativity in their professional practice provide creative possibilities that encourage students to utilize these same methods in their own learning process. Finally, the researchers state that "A pedagogy that fosters creativity may also actively involve the child in the determination of what knowledge is to be investigated and acquired, ensuring children a significant amount of control and opportunities to be innovative" (44). Professional development utilizing imagination promotes transformative learning. Transformative learning, as defined by Mezirow, "involves how to think critically about assumptions supporting one's perspectives and to develop critically reflective judgment in discourse regarding one's beliefs, values, feelings, and self-concepts" (2009, 29). Imagination is the process of envisioning "how things could be otherwise" and is the central component in initiating transformative learning (Mezirow 2009, 28). Play and inquiry are synonymous in many aspects. Wondering, imagining, and seeking are all significant components of play as well as inquiry. Einstein has been attributed with saying that play is the highest form of research. Thus, play is the perfect context or state of being to promote, implement, and support a deep inquiry approach to learning content and process, as we see illustrated in the following in-depth case study.

Case Study: *Improving Professional Development and Classroom Practice within Manatee County School District, Florida*

Researched and written by Michelle Compton and Beth Severson while serving as early childhood specialists within the Manatee County Public Schools, this rigorous in-depth study of the applied practice of self active play in professional development identifies clear and compelling evidence of how and why self active play protocols inspire teachers to improve instructional practice in their Pre-K early childhood classrooms.

The Beginning: Why Self Active Play?

During the 2015–2016 school year, the Manatee County School District's Early Learning Department was embarking on a new initiative to implement project work curriculum in pre-kindergarten classrooms that our team of early learning specialists developed collaboratively with teachers. The goal of the initiative was to provide a curriculum that integrated all standards with a particular focus on the integration of science and social studies standards and concepts. This initiative was important because the National Science Teachers Association released a position statement endorsed by the National Association for the Education of Young Children (NAEYC). It affirmed that learning science and engineering practices in the early years can foster children's curiosity and enjoyment in exploring the world around them and lay the foundation for a progression of science learning in the K–12 setting. Our goal was to lead teachers toward in-depth exploration experiences rooted in play. In this case study, the self active play professional development was designed to carefully promote creativity, imagination and play in all areas of the curriculum. As a result of the professional development, the early childhood teachers began implementing a new inquiry-based project curriculum. The professional development was intentionally designed to support the teachers as they created their curriculum around the "Building and Structures" inquiry project (Chalufour & Worth 2004).

The Teachers and Curriculum: Our Story

These forty-one teachers that our Early Learning Department supports have varying educational backgrounds that range from certified teachers to those with Child Development Associate (CDA) certificates. In partnership with classroom teachers, paraprofessionals also attended the trainings. In this way, collaborative teams were developed and subsequently planned together. The programs serve a diverse population of students, ranging from high poverty to affluence. The district identifies PreK classrooms according to two categories: Voluntary Pre-Kindergarten (VPK) classrooms that serve typically developing children and Integrated PreK (IPK) classrooms that include up to six students with special needs alongside typically developing students.

The teachers and specialists researched and designed an inquiry cycle applied during the planning, teaching, and learning of the in-depth investigations on the topics of nature, water, buildings and structures, as well as light and shadows. The phases of inquiry in our cycle were:

Phase 1: Engaging and Exploring

Phase 2: Taking Action and Making Sense

Phase 3: Learning With and From Each Other

However, providing an inquiry cycle with accompanying curriculum documents would not have provided enough support. The specialists also needed to provide ongoing professional development with the teachers in order to ensure the curriculum would come alive, especially as teachers began to use self active play experiences. Throughout implementation of the new curriculum, we realized that by applying the connected stages of our inquiry cycle to self active play experiences, students and teachers learned much more than the science and social studies concepts in their project work.

The Professional Development:
Self Active Play Education

During the spring of 2016, in collaboration with Dr. Walter Drew,

Manatee County's Early Learning Department launched the Curriculum Academy for Unit Three. The objective of unit three's project work was for students to play and build with materials in order to express their ideas and come to new understandings about their community and world. Dr. Drew agreed to host an adult play workshop using his blocks, which had been purchased for teachers along with a variety of loose recycled parts. Since self active education begins with sensory integration, the touching of physical objects, teachers were given the opportunity for free exploration with just Dr. Drew's Discovery Blocks. The teachers and paraprofessionals were involved in a solitary process of building with the blocks, no talking allowed. The teachers and paraprofessionals made the connection that phase one of the inquiry cycle is all about open-ended play. They realized the self active play encounter allows the child to explore and imagine how to use the materials in different ways, just as the adults experienced their play experience. You will see in the teachers' journal responses after the play session, the emergence of the adults' understanding of the importance and value of giving children the opportunity to engage in open-ended play.

Dr. Drew then led participants through a cooperative play experience and added additional loose parts and recycled materials, including red and yellow plastic caps of varying sizes and purple foam cylinders from the Reusable Resources Adventure Center. This time teachers were free to interact, problem solve, and work together to create an idea or project. The room was buzzing as teachers began designing and constructing their shared goals and visions of their structure. All voices were heard and there was time for negotiation of ideas so everyone contributed and felt valued. The reflective journal responses described the importance and appreciation of working with others and highlighted the need to persevere when the group was faced with a problem, such as how to rectify an unstable structure. These, of course, are the describing elements of Stage 2 of the self active education process; but they are also reflected in the in-depth investigations students would encounter during phase 2 of our inquiry process.

During this phase of the inquiry cycle, teachers lead their students into focused investigation lessons as they study and problem solve a topic of interest. These are the very experiences that we want teachers to employ as they guide students through learning, not only about buildings and structures, but investigating any topic in any content area.

Finally, teachers were given reflection time once again to think about their play experiences and how these experiences could impact their teaching of Unit Three. This reflection made by the teachers mirrored the final phase of our inquiry cycle when we asked the children to share their newly constructed learning as well as connect that new learning to the big ideas of the study. We want children to discover and share, "Why is this learning important?" This questioning stance sometimes leads children, with the support of the teacher, to create an action plan to put their changed or new thinking into practice.

Participants' Personal Responses: Emergent Themes in Solo Play

When reading and synthesizing the teachers' responses to the solitary play activity, overwhelmingly, participants were committed to building as an act of discovery requiring assertiveness and of bringing their imaginative ideas into reality. Consistent with the process of science inquiry and characteristics of play, many participants initiated the building task by physically interacting with the materials without a fully developed intention for their structures. Instead, intention formation evolved and became increasingly refined as they explored ideas as a consequence of physically interacting with the blocks. Other teachers commented that they began building with a clear vision or plan, though the plan had to be revised, reworked, and reimagined as problems arose. In early learning classrooms it is not uncommon to see teachers launch learning stations or center time activities according to a linear construct, inviting students to make a plan before going to a center, carry out plans, and meet for whole-class reflection. The self active play of adults in building structures provided the players with evidence that the non-linear, fluid processes of exploration and discovery, problem-solving and building intentionality, and reflection and synthesis characterize the self active education experience.

A theme that emerged as necessary for achieving agency and creativity was the open-ended nature of the tasks. This condition facilitated a sense of autonomy that was both motivating and liberating for uninhibited self-expression. Participants engaged with building as a personal act of discovery that was free from pressure or constraint. Inspiration to express or represent the content and meaning of their constructions came from personal experiences, such as gardening or vacationing. Some participants found inspiration from their professional experiences, considering topics their students were exploring in the classroom. Other participants described the inspiration they drew from the creative endeavors of their peers.

Finally, many participants described the way the materials and resources fostered, inhibited, or influenced the design of the structure and their creative agency. Resources were mentioned consistently as helping or hindering project development, such as the shapes, sizes, feel, and availability of the blocks to the cloth table coverings. Having *"enough blocks to choose from"* was particularly important and stimulated reflection among teachers on materials in their own classrooms.

The following response stood out as it highlighted stages of self active education, in addition to the components of the inquiry process, as this learner shares her progression from open exploration to more in-depth investigation.

> *"While building, it allowed me to focus on my thoughts of what I wanted my structure to look like. Doing it alone allowed me to problem solve, investigate, and explore the structure in my thoughts and put it into action with the blocks. More than being able to construct freely without interruption was the complete quiet (minus relaxing music), but not talking to others, allowed complete focus and problem solving without interruptions. It was nice to look around and see how everyone built something completely different."*

The following response truly captured the essence and importance of these types of professional development opportunities for teachers...True ownership, lessons learned, and sense of pride! This was yet another connection teachers made to the stages of self active play and the phases of the inquiry cycle. Describing the problems they encountered and the use of persistence to create their structures mirrored students' descriptions of their learning processes, problem-solving, and sequences of persistence during "builder's talks."

> "I was able to build with no pressure. I was free to be creative and use my own skills, create whatever was in my mind in that moment. I wanted to be me, and create something different than anybody else, be unique. I feel like I made mistakes but I learned by my mistakes. At the end I was proud of my creation because it was mine. I made it. I feel like it's part of me."

Participants' Responses:
Emergent Themes in Cooperative Play

In response to the cooperative play activities, several emergent themes were congruent with the responses to the solitary play task. Other themes emerged from the responses that were unique and reflected the benefits and challenges of group interaction during cooperative open-ended block play. The themes *fun* and *problem solving*, for example, were reflected in both the solitary and cooperative experiences.

When working with peers, responses collectively demonstrated the ways participants strived toward and celebrated creative collaboration. Teachers used words like *fun, helpful, awesome*, and *engaging* when describing the social learning environment. Participants alluded to the synergistic effects of coming together in an atmosphere of play and the heightened sense of connection and accomplishment that resulted as evidenced by the following statements:

- *I felt a sense of comradery toward the group. I wanted to keep playing.*

- *Working together makes it better!*

- *This was purely creative collaboration and FUN among friends. Sheer social skills and creating.*

- *I think creating with a group was a more fulfilling and rich experience.*

Along with the sense of connection and accomplishment, three other themes emerged from the cooperative play experience, each characterizing the essential necessity to achieve creative collaboration: *the evolution and transformation of thinking to identify a shared goal, negotiating individual and group identity, and persistence.* Many teachers began their written responses by identifying the group's intention and the role of negotiation when envisioning and planning the project. Closely connected with this theme was frequent transformation of ideas. In other words, structures typically started off as one thing and during the cooperative play experience evolved into something else. Some participants actively engaged in the exchange of ideas while others participated more actively in the construction of the project. Identifying a shared purpose seemed an important goal for participants to conquer early on and was, at times, a point of tension or frustration. The identification of a shared goal seemed necessary for the manifestation of *joy, humor, a sense of empowerment, spontaneity, and fun* – all characteristics essential to play.

A second theme consistently articulated was the negotiation of individual and group identities. An important part of the experience for teachers was to participate as an individual in a way that productively contributed to the group's shared vision. Also a point of tension at times, some reported their struggle to determine their role within the group. This was inhibiting for some while others eased in quickly as active contributors to the group. The feeling of coming together and achieving group *flow* contributed significantly to teachers experiencing joy with the task. Where *flow* is defined as a peak experience with a heightened state of consciousness experienced during challenging, intrinsically motivating tasks (Csikszentmihalyi 1996), *group flow* describes an experience when the group is performing with heightened effectiveness (Sawyer 2008). Listening, role identification, and participation are group behaviors that set the stage for attaining group flow and are consistent with the content of participants' responses.

A third theme also evident in the solitary play experience, though more prevalent here, was persistence. Many teachers reported feeling that the group project was enhanced and heightened by the social interaction and the contributions of all group members. To achieve this heightened sense of experience required persistence – sticking to it when problems arose. Limited resources, role identification, faulty plans, and falling blocks were problematic for groups and points of tension, though participants explained how they persisted in order to "get it right."

The following is an example of one of the adult responses that mirrors what we see when the students construct a project together and share their learning.

"Everyone's ideas contributing to the creativity – when one person suggested something it would trigger an idea in another. Then that idea triggered another and so on...great creative brainstorming while constructing. I liked that no one person controlled the construction but that all persons contributed and even adjusted their own thinking for the good of the structure. Working together makes it better!"

This next example highlights the doubt that some participants felt using this kind of "play" experience and reveals the need for specialists to support teachers by providing these types of experiences, thus, enabling the participants to realize why and how to implement similar experiences with their students.

"At first I wasn't sure six of us could actually work together. I had my own vision of what I wanted to do but had to take into consideration what the group wanted. Once we got going it was so much fun sharing ideas and listening to the others' ideas. I felt a release of stress as we were working, "playing". Also felt comradery toward the group. I want to keep playing!."

Teachers' Post-Workshop Reflection Survey

We surveyed the teachers after the training to fully document the synthesis stage of self active play. *Did they change how they felt about play in their classroom? How did this experience impact their professional practice?* The responses were inspiring. Engaging in play reminded adults about the importance of play in their classrooms. Many had forgotten what it felt like to play and did not realize how play could stimulate creativity and imagination. When asked about the most impactful experience during the adult play workshop, participants reflected:

- *Getting to play with the blocks and feeling what it feels like to play and build again. When the blocks I built up fell down, I thought about what I say to my students, "It's okay, you can build them better/stronger next time." That thought encouraged me to try again and indeed, the next building was stronger.*

- *The block play session gave me the opportunity to "play." It enabled me the opportunity to see through the eyes of my students as they explore with new materials. I was able to work cooperatively with peers toward a common goal and be creative.*

- *When I first looked at Dr. Drew's Blocks I thought, "They are all the same." But it is amazing what you can build.*

- *First, seeing the creativity of the different structures being built. Then, watching what adding another element brought to those structures. And hearing all the stories emerging as the building was brought to life.*

Even though play had a role in their classrooms, it had now become a necessary component as teachers designed learning engagements and investigations for the teaching of mathematics, literacy, science, and social studies. More time was given to play! More lessons were created with play experiences in the forefront of planning. Many teachers synthesized their learning by describing how their teaching had changed based on the adult play workshop:

- *I encouraged the children in the beginning of our study to experiment with individual learning with the blocks, with music in the background to stimulate their creativity. I also did this again as one of the culminating activities, along with sketching their structures.*

- *The adult play workshop showed me the importance of 'letting go' and allowing my students to express themselves without my interference. I was really impressed how easily my students accepted the 'quiet' work time. Seeing their reactions and the quality of their work changed my way of thinking and how I respond to their work.*

- *We gave our students more open exploration time with blocks. We saw what the children could learn from playing with blocks. They built towers, castles, and homes. We also added drawing their work for their own documentation.*

- *I have included a lot more 'silent' activities in my class. It's a way to make them a little more creative. To make decisions based upon what they want to do, not what their friends/classmates or teacher want them to do.*

- *I took pictures of the buildings and work being done to show my students and inspire them. I have also added other materials to the block area. I began using their buildings as a beginning to a story for them to tell and draw.*

Insights by the Specialists for Early Learning, (Michelle and Beth)

Michelle Compton Response
When learning and experiencing the stages of the self active education during the adult play workshop, I was really surprised by how

much it mirrored the phases of inquiry that we had developed with our teachers. These self active education stages reflect the natural process of learning. They lay the foundation for creativity, imagination, and innovation to occur. We engaged first in open exploration and play with materials as described in both Stage One of self active education and Phase One of the inquiry cycle. Likewise, we made sense and further investigated a particular topic as outlined in Stage or Phase Two of both processes. Finally, we reflected and made action plans to improve teaching practices and to promote differences in our own lives similar to Stage Three and Phase Three. By engaging in inquiry through authentic play experiences we discovered new possibilities within ourselves and our worlds.

In just a few days after the adult play workshop, I witnessed teachers planning opportunities for both solitary and collaborative learning engagements, allowing children to explore the blocks in different ways. Most teachers were surprised at how long their early learners actually focused and built in a quiet environment, while listening to music playing softly in the background. They witnessed their students fully focused as they employed all their senses to explore the different types of blocks and carefully make their choices of materials as their creativity led them into building their structures.

I was also reminded about the importance of making time for reflection throughout our study with students. Many teachers created new spaces in their classrooms to supply their students with clipboards and paper so they could sketch their structures and reflect on what they had built.

Finally, I was fascinated during the adult play workshop by the natural progression of participants' talk, creating dialogue and stories to explain the structures they had built. I had been noticing this with students during my action research project I had initiated earlier this year, but didn't realize that, even as adults, when working with materials in an open-ended manner it unlocks memories and stories that we want to share and tell to others. This continues to be the heart and passion of my research: to show we can share ways for teachers to use play and open-ended materials to unlock the stories in children's minds and hearts. Learning across all domains is evidenced in the stories the children find, build, and share as they engage in self active play.

Beth Severson Response

When observing the self active education experience unfold within the context of professional development, two things stood out as significant. First, when teachers participated in the solitary play with blocks, they were actively engaged in a state of relaxed alertness for a much longer period of time than I might have predicted. Each seemed motivated, curious, and focused—able to achieve a state of equipoise or balance. When I reflected with teachers immediately following the activity, many enthusiastically described the variety of ways they would transfer this independent learning experience to their classrooms, and they acknowledged independent building was something they hadn't considered implementing. They explained that their students often built with others, but they hadn't provided the time nor had they created the atmosphere for students to build autonomously. In one classroom I visited after the workshop, a teacher implemented several independent experiences mimicking the workshop experience. "So many more kids are choosing to go to blocks now," she told me. "Look at Alora. She is a master-builder now and she never chose to go to blocks before!" Merging the independent and collaborative building tasks heightened the experience for teachers and they transferred these experiences to their classrooms.

Second, I was particularly intrigued with the different ways teachers constructed meaning during and following building activities. Noteworthy was the way descriptions of their structures contained elements of narration. When Dr. Drew prompted, "Tell us about your structure," individuals and groups often laid the groundwork for storytelling by establishing an elaborate setting, such as a resort with spaces for different family members described as a day unfolds or by connecting the structure to a story from their past, e.g. "When I was little I would go camping and we would..." In the professional development session, Dr. Drew included video of a session where he enacted solitary building experience with young learners, and I noted the narrative elements in students' responses including descriptions of settings, characters, references to conflicts, and utilization of narrative grammatical forms. (See YouTube Link in the appendix.) The relationship between thought, play, and the projection of story seemed an important topic for further investigation.

Lessons Learned

There were many lessons learned, both during and after the adult play workshop. By participating in each stage of the self active play experience, it was evident that play and inquiry are synonymous in many ways. All learners, no matter their topic of study, always begin in a wondering and imaginative stage. They need to have the time, space, and materials to actively explore and engage in their play experiences without preconceived outcomes. This process takes time, but if we carefully watch the students, we will notice their interests come alive. We observed students returning to the same material again and again, indicating to us their continued and deep curiosity about a particular material or learning experience we had established.

It is critical to embed many self-reflective activities through-out all stages of the inquiry process so that students can evaluate their learning and create new pathways for investigation. As was mentioned previously, Einstein said, "Play is the highest form of re-search." Teachers learned to provide focused investigation lessons, such as building challenges to create a tower. They also learned to provide students with open-ended materials for play, enabling the children to find and build stories. No matter the topic, children used materials creatively to research and find the answers to many of their wonderings.

As specialists, we were reminded of the importance of provid-ing professional development sessions for the teachers that mirror the philosophical underpinnings, instructional methods, and in-quiry-based explorations we expect teachers to provide for their students. We believe the inquiry process necessitates grounding in-vestigations through play; therefore, the agenda and materials we provide during professional development workshops must actively engage participants in the same stages of wondering, reflection, and synthesis. Teachers must experience open-ended explorations, using the same materials the children will explore. It is important for teachers to connect to play, reflect on their experiences, consider problems children might face, and collaboratively work together to imagine things they had not anticipated.

We are moving forward as a collaborative group of teachers and specialists, applying the lessons we learned during the adult play workshop. It is most beneficial to remember the importance and value of play as we build new experiences for the children that we serve because this is how humans learn. This is how we wonder. This is how we investigate. And this is how we reflect and grow as a community of learners!

CONCLUSION

THIS CHAPTER HIGHLIGHTS the importance of high-quality professional development in order to improve educators' professional practice. The perspective and evidence cited in the extraordinary case study with Manatee County Pre-K teachers clearly exemplifies the value of using hands-on, solitary and cooperative self active play as a professional development strategy for strengthening creativity, imagination, and storytelling in the classroom. The self active play process has been used successfully in multiple contexts with similar positive professional transformations. Inspired by their own self active play experience, teachers make the connection with children's learning and discover creative ways of applying this play process in the classroom.

Chapter 5

Expanding the Possibilities and Benefits of Self Active Play

"When we stop playing, we stop developing, and when that happens, the laws of entropy take over – things fall apart. Ultimately, we share the fate of the sea squirt and become vegetative, staying in one spot, not fully interacting with the world, more plant than animal. When we stop playing, we start dying."

—Stuart Brown, (2009, p. 73)

WHEN PEOPLE THINK of play, they typically associate it with the experiences of young children. However, Erickson (1997) established the value of play across the human lifespan and as an essential process for coping with the aging process. While our previous chapters focused on the benefits of self active play for children and the adults who work with them, in this chapter we want to broaden the story to examine the impact of play on older adults playing alone, with other adults, and with members of a different generation.

We examined data from a retirement home study, a case study with an older adult suffering from Alzheimer's disease, and the value of intergenerational play. We share our results with you through the stories that follow.

The Story: *Quality of Life*

Research into the aging process includes looking at quality of life issues that affect how older adults experience their later years. Like play, quality of life is studied in many different fields and therefore draws on different understandings from each. We consider quality-of-life skills to be those that enable the older adult or elder to function and be part of their chosen experiences and the life around them. Stamina, sense of balance, and physical dexterity change over time, as do social circles and living circumstances. Adapting to those physical changes in order to stay engaged with personal interests requires the ability to focus, organize, and be flexible in order to stay active and involved. These are strong indicators of quality of life.

Self active play is an ideal context in which to develop and strengthen physical dexterity as well as mental flexibility as players handle materials, play and experiment with possibilities. We've come to understand the benefits of self active play as a way for older adults to maintain and develop neuroplasticity, a sense of creative purpose and personal accomplishment, and appreciate change as a positive force for confirming one's possibilities. Learning to accept and deal with change is a vital component of quality of life.

The journal reflections of participants have often indicated that mental stress is released when the adult plays quietly as soft music plays in the background. During silent solitary play with open-ended materials, players unwind, destress, and let go of daily concerns. The use of reusable materials donated by local businesses adds a unique depth to the knowledge gained during the play. In materials initially put aside and deemed unworthy of anything but the landfill, players find beauty and delight. In experiencing this, retirees who feel cast off by their workplaces may find in the new works of art created from repurposed materials a metaphor of hope and new possibilities, a new purpose.

The Story: *Cross Keys Village Retirement Home*

One of our case studies examined self active play with retirees living in a retirement community, Cross Keys. We've shared this research at conferences, and it is included in a chapter of *Play and Culture*, volume 13, published in 2016 by The Association for the Study of Play (TASP). Our understanding of the importance of play in the lives of older adults and elders was confirmed during this research study. In the reflective journals and subsequent interviews with the participants, the data clearly supported *Principle 2: hands-on play and art making with open-ended materials reconnect the individual with earlier stages of human development, spontaneously balancing and strengthening, hope, will, purpose, competence, fidelity, love, care, and wisdom.*

During the play experience, the participants identified memories from their past that resonated with different components of the play workshop. For example, during a self active play experience using tempera paints, one participant, who had recently suffered from a stroke, reminisced about her time at the beach as a little girl. Using her painting as a prop, she brightened as she shared her childhood beach experiences recalling times when she took her own children to the beach. Her entire facial expression changed as she spoke about those memories, which had surfaced in her consciousness through her play experience.

Another resident, Betty, was mentally fit but had physical impairment. She was confined to a wheelchair and unable to use her hands. Betty attended the play workshop and was accompanied by a personal aide. During the painting session, Betty chose the colors and directed her assistant to make specific brush strokes on the paper. Then Betty decided she wanted to do the painting herself, so her aide placed the brush between her teeth and Betty manipulated it on the paper to create a part of her painting. Betty smiled happily and with a look of satisfaction after painting. She was grateful for the chance to take part in "playing with paints." Betty also told stories from her past that were ignited during her play. She shared how she and her husband had traveled to the Greek islands, where they spent hours on the beach, *"watching sunrises and the glistening light shimmering across the water."* She asked us as we admired her painting, "Do you like my Van Gogh? He painted *A Starry Night* and I painted *A Sunny Day!*"

The self active play process holds great promise for supporting positive quality of life for older adults. After this experience, the director for community life at Cross Keys shared, "A huge 'Thank You' to Dr. Marcia Nell and Dr. Walter Drew for allowing our residents to participate in a project that gives them a feeling of 'self-worth.' Sometimes we forget just what talents we still have if we are never given a chance to use them."

The Story: *George and the Paints*

Our second elder case study was with George, age eighty-four, who suffered from Alzheimer's disease. His symptoms included idle wandering, fidgeting, and forgetfulness. It was not unusual for George to wander around the house, anxiously looking out the windows, as if he were expecting someone or something. George was a retired businessman and had kept busy since his early retirement by working at various maintenance jobs for his retirement condominium association. As the disease progressed, he became more and more anxious. George would watch TV, but as he did so he plucked at the arms of his easy chair until the upholstery was shredded and frayed. His wife, Lucy, was his primary caregiver and spent much of her time caring for George. However, caregiving duties were becoming harder and harder for Lucy to manage on her own. She was on constant watch to be sure George was safe.

Our time with George and Lucy began with a silent solo play session using watercolor paints. George and Lucy both participated in the art play session. Soothing music played in the background as they painted. Typically, we allot approximately twenty minutes for a silent solo play session. This time, with George's history of fidgeting and restlessness, we decided not to time the session but rather to let George engage with the paints until he showed signs of being finished with the play. As George and Lucy sat around their kitchen table, George interacted with the brush, paper, and paints for over eighty minutes. He did not have a background in the arts, according to Lucy, nor had he shown any interest in them as a younger man. During the play, George stayed focused and didn't ask for clarification on what he was supposed to do. He simply engaged with the paints for the full eighty minutes. For George, this time was filled with purpose, creative activity, and relief from his anxiety.

During that eighty minutes of focused painting, Lucy was relieved of her constant watching of George. Because George stayed in his seat and played with the paints, Lucy was able to relax as well. She noted in discussions afterward that it would be important to give George an opportunity to play with paints again, especially on days when he was particularly agitated and anxious. George has passed away as of this writing, but his case study has powerful implications for implementation of non-pharmaceutical strategies for patients with Alzheimer's disease and the benefits of such interventions for caregivers.

Intergenerational Play

Dr. Edgar Klugman, professor emeritus of Wheelock College and co-creator of the National Association for the Education of Young Children's Play, Policy and Practice Interest Forum, reflected on play:

"At age 84, I cannot face any activity that does not have embedded in it a playful approach to the task that provides me

with fun, joy, good feelings, challenges and oftentimes is ac-
companied by new learnings—like when I explore and play
with materials I've never seen or touched before or learning
to text my grandchildren in order to keep in touch. In the
event it is not, I will make it playful. There are times when
I am playing that I experience feelings and thoughts I've
never had before and reminisce."

(Nell, Drew, Klugman, Jones & Cooper, 2010, 3)

In thinking of the playful activities of his later years, he high-lighted how finding the joy in a potentially troublesome task, learn-ing to use text messaging, connected him with his youngest grand-daughter, then working in a restaurant in Italy. He also saw it as a potential alternative to more physical play as his body was less able to join in playing catch with his grandchildren. He concluded, "Young, middle aged, mature, and older learn to appreciate each other in new ways and how we can be together and play together both in virtual and real space" (2010, 3). Play thus creates a bridge between generations, enabling them to find common ground for communicating and relating to each other.

Klugman's words remind us of a parent who shared that her teenage son was going through a typical stage of development by pulling back from the family. She felt estranged from her son and longed for the days when they would spend time together playing and enjoying each other's company. As she reminisced about her son's younger years, the memories sparked an idea to try to recon-nect with her son through one of their favorite ways of spending time together when he was younger: playing with blocks. She re-trieved the set of blocks from the attic and laid them out on the floor in the place where they used to spend hours together, building towers and castles and lavish stories of possibilities. Sure enough, her son gravitated toward the blocks, sat down, and began to fiddle with them. Soon he was absorbed in the building, and she slid in be-side him and began to play with the blocks, too. They reconnected in part because of the strong play history they had shared when her son was younger.

Reflections on Mixed-Age Play in Theory and Practice

Dr. James Johnson, distinguished professor at The Pennsylvania State University, shared with us his insight into the concept of mixed-age play. He highlights the value of providing children of different ages with the opportunity to play together.

Self active cooperative play experiences offer an ideal opportunity for children of different ages and adults to play and learn new skills together, skills that promote social and emotional development, along with cognitive and language development. In mixed-age play, Vygotsky's zone of proximal development occurs spontaneously between the younger and older children. An ideal context for such self active play is after-school programs, where children can be encouraged to engage in mixed-age play experiences. Mixed-age play could also be promoted in early childhood and primary classrooms through the thoughtful and intentional planning of teachers who understand and value this idea. Family engagement programs and even individual families with children of different ages are likewise prime partners for promoting mixed-age play.

Play energizes people at all ages, and social play brings added value. Special added value comes with age-mixed play, often defined as play by peers fourteen or more months apart. Cross-age peer relations can happen when groups of young children are together in school, home and community settings.

The dynamics of cross-age peer relations versus same-age interaction have been studied for many years, with its evolutionary-adaptive benefits noted (Konner, 1975). Gray (2011; "Special Value," 2013) argues that the freedom of different age children to mingle together at play and other activities goes far back in human evolutionary history to hunter-gatherer societies. Children had greater freedom to play and learn in natural habitats prior to the age of agriculture, and a few such societies still exist: roving bands with twenty to fifty persons of all ages roaming territories seeking game and vegetation.

Their life-style necessitates learning as coequals without competition and with sharing and respect for each other. Such an existence helped humans evolve the ability to educate themselves in social commerce with varied-aged individuals. From this historical-evolutionary perspective, Gray (2013, 182) notes "the segregation of children by age is an oddity—I would say a tragic oddity—of modern times."

Regrettably, today's children have limited opportunities to play across age divisions. This state of affairs is done for the convenience of adults, not with children's perspectives and best interests in mind. When children are age-segregated, like they are in the typical classroom and in after-school sports and activities organized by adults, they are deprived of exercising adaptive skills for autonomous learning and caring. Their freedom is curtailed.

Early childhood education experts agree on the advantages of mixed-age programming (Katz, Evangelou, & Hartman, 1990). Mixed age is a leading standard of high quality according to OMEP, the World Organization of Early Childhood Education. Benefits accrue to children from the chances to interact with younger and older peers. Older children gain from opportunities to fine-tune their social radars as they make accommodative shifts while playing with younger children, and younger children learn from and can be nurtured by older role models. For example, consider a simple bout of kicking a soccer ball back and forth. Two younger children trying this could fail, comically perhaps. An older child scaffolding this play bout, mediating the novices' play intentions and actions, would gradually improve the younger children's performance over time while also learning to be a better teacher. Younger children accept older children as helpful leaders and instructors. Older children see younger ones as in need of their care and tutelage. Katz, Evangelou, and Hartman aptly stated that children of different ages tap into each other's zones of proximal development, especially during collaborative play. Mixed-age programs are developmentally appropriate, "whole child" learning programs par excellence.

Teachers can better harness the power of mixed-age play by increasing their knowledge and mindful use of facilitation strategies. A good example is reported by Roopnarine and Bright (1993). For three consecutive years (1978–80) they directed a summer university program for children from three to eight years of age in Madison, Wisconsin. They focused on including teachers as researchers as they planned and implemented large and small group activities in language and communication, arts and crafts, dance and movement, dramatic play, and science and nature. The researchers, along with the research teachers, sought and achieved increasing knowledge about how to give the children ample opportunities for observational learning, imitation, and play tutoring. Teachers devised and studied situations, such as making a wall mural or planning a carnival, that elicited engagement in simple to complex modes of cognitive and social play involving same-age and cross-age peers.

The University of Wisconsin social individual model of mixed-age socialization was successful in demonstrating children's attraction to children older and younger than themselves. Older girls were very keen on playing with younger children; this trend was seen consistently over the three years. Older boys also exhibited cross-age play, but not as much as same-age play; the younger boys showed more play with older boys. Overall, teachers became increasingly effective in using materials, arranging activities, and supervising and encouraging age-mixed group participation and cohesion, avoiding didactic teaching and age segregation of the children.

The Story: *Family Block Play Workshop: Promoting Mixed Age Play Between Children and Family Members*

In 2015, the United Way Center for Excellence in Early Education, Miami, Florida, hosted an end-of-the-year "family play night" during the Week of the Young Child. The ninety-minute family play workshop with Dr. Drew brought thirty-five children and adults together to play on with purple foam cylinders, red and yellow plastic caps, and Dr. Drew's Discovery Blocks. Marbles and plastic ball runs were available for the older children to use on two large tables. After a brief welcome introduction, the children and parents were invited to explore the material and go with the "flow" of creative play. Most of the play took place on a wooden floor in a room surrounded by a wall of mirrors and window.

The primary goal of the workshop was for the parents and children to engage in play together, to be free to explore and build together with abundant materials. The players were free to make choices and discoveries on their own. They were focused and fully engaged in exploring, discovering, and spontaneously expressing themselves creatively through constructive play with open-ended materials. Parents enjoyed playtime with their children and deepened their understanding of why self active play with open-ended materials is so important to the healthy development of children and family life in general. Parents were encouraged to observe and think about the positive outcome of playing together with their children. The following comment illustrates some of the benefits of self active play as seen by the father through playing with his son:

> *"It's really nice when you are with your son and see him use his imagination and creativity. I observed him excited and engaged in thinking about design and structure. The experience was very thought provoking for me and for him. I almost didn't come to the workshop but really glad I did."*

> —Father attending the workshop.

All around the room were examples of elaborate thinking in the form of "a castle," "farm," "towers," and "marble runs." It was fun to see two fathers jump in and play together to create a huge curving "dominoes run." There were cheers and laughter as the blocks fell one after another! It was inspiring to see children and parents freely playing together as they imagine, build, and create structures, thoughts and questions and solutions to problems that are of immediate interest to them. As a way of documenting the experience, parents were asked to reflect and share their impressions of the evening.

One of the fathers shared:

"If parents can allow themselves to exist in this exciting play state it benefits the children."

One four-year-old boy reflected and shared,

"This is a tower, and it is rigid. My mother and I made it together."

His obvious appreciation of making a tower together with his mother and his choice of the word *rigid* are unmistakably rich with personal meaning. Next to this pair, another child and his father sat

together constructing the whole time. They talked and created a series of changing structures, aesthetically assembled and then transformed them into something completely different.

After the event, Paula Moujalli, the center's principal and director, offered her critique of the family evening of play. She noted:

> "It was very interesting to see the interactions between the families who attended, parents and their children, and children with other children. We noticed how the families had the opportunity to engage as a community. We also saw the value of taking time to demonstrate the use of the open-ended materials and how they could be used as tools to help guide meaningful interactions."

Feedback on the event was very positive.

As Peter Gray and Brian Sutton Smith both said, play is an essential ingredient in healthy development, even a matter of survival. Just as with tiger cubs, kittens, and frolicking puppies, play builds capacity to survive and flourish, whether as an individual, a clan, or the whole human community. "It is a happy talent to know how to play", as Ralph Waldo Emerson once said. (Porte, Joel, 1982. *Emerson in His Journals*. The President and Fellows of Harvard College).

The Story: *Families Playing and Creating Art Together*

> "In a world where people are continually in a process of defining themselves and their communities, arts programs can be an integral part of building community...Intergenerational art programs emphasize exploring commonalities and differences and learning respect, tolerance, and appreciation through the art form."

—Susan Perlstein, Elders Share the Arts (Perlstein)

Maria Christina and Edward Pazzanese share their award-winning efforts of providing community-based play and art making experiences with children and adults of varying abilities, multicultural communities, and at risk-social groups in society. Families Creating Together (FCT) was founded in Jamaica Plain, MA, in 2008, and was inspired by "Elders Share the Arts" in New York City. The focus of FCT is to build communities of interest and leadership supporting play and art making in local educational and cultural institutions. The work of families Creating Together offers answers to the following questions: *How do play and arts programs contribute to the life and strength of a community? Who has access to neighborhood-based arts and play programs? How can we empower community members to make decisions and hold leadership positions in their educational and cultural organizations?* (Pazzanese, 1999).

The purpose of FCT is to build a sense of community within disenfranchised groups through the arts. At FCT, there is a significant effort to bring together those individuals who have typically been left out of the art community. During the creation of FCT, the needs assessment indicated that many of local programs did not include children with disabilities and their families into their arts programs. There was no provision for making inclusive environments for people with differing abilities. FCT programs and core principles embrace process-oriented art that encompasses self active play, inclusion, and the fostering of communication and community capacity-building.

FCT is a series of multi-week workshops using expressive art making to provide parents and caregivers the means of engaging families in creative play and the arts at home. FCT includes field trips to local art museums, science museums and other cultural institutions. Each of FCT's family art workshops highlights specific concepts such as seasons, imaginary creature, the life cycle and uses a variety of different art forms such as puppetry, painting, ceramics, fabric arts, or found objects. Each evening session includes dinner and provides the participants time to brainstorm and share ideas within the group.

As with self active play, the FTC program highlights the importance of process over the product. Linda Carol Edwards states:

"A process-oriented approach to the visual and performing arts involves a heightened sensitivity and awareness of what

you are doing while you are doing it. A product approach is more concerned with the final outcome or product, rather than with the experience of creating. When we are concerned about how our art compares with that of others, we are focusing on product. When we experiment and discover new ways to work with art materials or think of new and different ways to move our bodies to music, we are focusing on process."

(Edwards, 1997, p. 7)

It is through the play and the art making during the workshops that narrative storytelling arise during the reflective process used in self active play. Through the participants' sharing their stories, imagination and literacy development is encouraged. Co-creating family stories together gives children and adults experiences in expressive and receptive language skills. The families participate in cooperative play opportunities as a way of building self-esteem. Play and art making together help individuals develop a feeling of belonging and connection to their own family history and social community.

CONCLUSION

IN THIS CHAPTER, stories of self active play illustrate its positive impact on quality of life across the human lifespan. For example, self active play has encouraged positive engagement among residents of a retirement community and mitigated anxiety in an elder with Alzheimer's disease. Self active play is also a tool for connecting across generations, connecting grandparents with grandchildren and creating a quiet time in which parents and their children, and children of different ages, can connect authentically in a shared activity. The simple process of self active play has enormous power to bring together people of different ages, cultures, and life experiences. Whether learned in early childhood, as is ideal, or developed later in life, self active play offers many benefits across the entire human lifespan.

PART III

EXPANDING
SELF ACTIVE PLAY
BEYOND THE CLASSROOM

Chapter 6

Therapeutic Benefits of Self Active Play

"Play provides a singular opportunity to build the executive functioning that underlies adaptive behaviors at home; improve language and math skills in school; build the safe, stable, and nurturing relationships that buffer against toxic stress; and build social-emotional resilience."

—Yogman, M., Garner, A., Hutchinson, J.,
Hirsh-Pasek, K., Golinkoff, R. M., 2018 p. 11

IN THIS CHAPTER we share stories that highlight the therapeutic value of self active play, especially with children suffering from sudden traumatic loss and toxic stress. This form of play serves as an intervention for relieving suffering in the lives of children and adults. The child or the adult who experiences life circumstances, such as "abuse, neglect, caregiver substance abuse or mental illness, exposure to violence, family economic hardship without adequate adult support", can have life-long negative impact on the future happiness and well-being of that individual, that is, their ability to survive and flourish (Center on the Developing Child, Harvard University, p. 1).

The American Academy of Pediatrics Clinical Report includes specific recommendations that align with the foundational principles of self active play. The report emphasizes the importance of play in promoting healthy child development and maintaining the family-child bond. Self active play is intended to support and encourage healthy child development and family dynamics that have been disrupted through trauma and loss.

Restoring Hope Through Play—Therapeutic Playwork with Children in Transylvania

The first story we share is from Dr. Fraser Brown and his Playwork with the Roma children in Transylvania. The use of play was the primary tool used to help these children overcome their tragic living conditions and toxic stress. Dr. Brown's dramatic example of how play was used in a therapeutic process, but by no means, is this example limited to those children in Romania. Children around the world and in our own communities are suffering from poverty, violence, and oppression, while play is a universal tool that can be used for healing as a buffer against depression and suffering.

Self active play *Principle No. 1*, as stated by Nell, Drew, and Bush (2013, 7) suggests that *"Play is a source of creative energy, a positive force, and a safe context for constructing meaningful self-knowledge and revitalizing the human spirit across the continuum of the human life-cycle."* This very much reflects Sutton-Smith's (1999, 254) statement that "Players come out of their ludic paradoxes ... with renewed belief in the worthwhileness of merely living." The renowned play therapist Virginia Axline suggested that play is often a healing process and that *"children who are given unrestricted opportunities to play in a richly equipped playroom (with a non-threatening adult) are capable of solving their own emotional problems"* (Brown 2014, 78). When all these ideas are taken together, we have a powerful explanation for the developmental change that took place in the lives of the children who are the subject of the following piece: a group of chronically abused children in a Romanian pediatric hospital.

In the early part of 1999, the White Rose Initiative (WRI), a UK charity, was contacted by the new director of hospitals in Sighisoara, Dr. Cornell Puskas. On taking up his appointment he had been shown around the hospitals. During the tour he was taken to the pediatric hospital, where he discovered a ward with sixteen abandoned children, all tied into their cots. The children ranged in age from nine months to twelve years old, and all were awaiting transfer to children's mental hospitals, albeit (thankfully) there were no vacancies. All of the children were staring vacantly at nothing in particular, rocking gently, and making hardly a sound. It was impossible to tell which children had been born with some form of brain damage and which were merely the product of their abusive environment. Puskas was aware of Harlow's (1971) experiments with baby monkeys and his conclusion that no play makes for a very socially disturbed monkey. In fact, if the baby monkeys were reared in isolation but at the same time given time in a playroom with normally developing monkeys, they grew up to be relatively normal. The parallels between the life experience of these sixteen children and Harlow's isolate-reared monkeys were obvious. Puskas set aside a room to be used as a playroom and asked the WRI whether they could employ someone to play with the children. They did so and in turn asked the staff at Leeds Beckett University to offer some training for their new Romanian playworker, Edit Bus. That was the point at which I became involved, i.e., in organizing some very basic "on the job" training for Edit Bus in the United Kingdom.

Once Edit Bus returned to Romania, she became aware of additional deprivations: the children were not being fed properly; they were not bathed regularly; their diapers were changed no more than once a day; their ward was not kept clean; they had no sheets on their mattresses; and when they were sick, they were treated with shared needles, which was shocking because some of them were believed to be HIV positive. Their development was stunted in every way—the most extreme example being a ten-year-old boy who had the muscular-skeletal structure of a four-year-old. Fortunately, there was a nine-month-old toddler in the group who was relatively normal. That was a stroke of good fortune for the project, as he unwittingly became our equivalent of Harlow's "therapist monkey." In other words, his presence in the group clearly enabled some of the children to go back to the beginning and start their development again.

After Edit Bus had been working with the children for a couple of months, one of our students, Sophie Webb, went out to the hospital to complete the professional practice element of her Playwork degree course. Here is an extract from Webb's reflective diary that nicely captures the plight of the children:

"These were my first impressions of the conditions at the hospital and the way the children are treated:

"The silence. Every room was full of children in cots, but it was so quiet. Even when we entered the room there was no sound from the children. They just looked at us. The smell of urine in every room was almost unbearable. The emptiness. Each room had just the cots with plastic mattresses. The children were dirty and wearing clothes that were too big for them. Some were wearing jumpers [sweaters] as trousers, and none of them were wearing shoes. There were rags around their waists, which I later found out were ripped up sheets, tied to keep the nappies [diapers] in place. These rags were also used to tie the children to the cots. Most children were sitting, rocking, and others were standing up banging the sides of their cots against the walls. Giving the children a cuddle was strange as they either held on too tightly or they remained stiff and unfeeling.

"When I observed the children in the playroom, they were unaware of each other, fixed on their own activities—barely communicating. Some just sat and seemed bewildered and vacant."

It is hard to imagine a more disadvantaged and routinely abused group of children outside of a war zone. Yet despite all that, every child was able to make remarkable progress—even those who had clearly been born with some form of identifiable brain damage. Indeed, some of the children made a degree of developmental progress that none of us expected. They moved through Freud's (1905) psychosexual stages of development in double quick time. It was as

though they just needed to make a good connection with a stage before moving on towards the stage that might be considered appropriate to their particular age. The more able children were engaging in complex and abstract forms of symbolic play within four months of entering the WRI's Therapeutic Playwork Project. According to Piaget (1951) symbolic play takes between two and three years to develop, and abstract cognition appears towards the end of that period. How was it that these children made such striking progress in such a short period of time?

Our playworkers had to untie the children in the morning, bathe them, feed them properly, work with them in the playroom all day, and then take them back to the ward in the evening, where the nurses would tie them to their cots again. They would then receive no human attention until the playworkers arrived in the morning. In other words, nothing changed in the lives of these children other than their experience of the WRI project. Thus, it is possible to say that any developmental change was a direct consequence of their experience of the Therapeutic Playwork Project. Clearly the children were now being treated with kindness and fed properly. However, although that may account for the more relaxed mood of the children, it is unlikely their development was a direct result of those factors. On the contrary, we became convinced that interactive social play was the most significant factor in achieving change. In other words, the major catalyst in bringing about change was the playful environment we created, rather than any specific work undertaken with individual children. That is not to under-value the specific techniques that were employed at times to help individual children. Nevertheless, the strongest influence on the children's development was undoubtedly the children themselves. Their engagement with each other was a joy to behold and left no doubt in our minds that play is indeed the "safe context for con-structing meaningful self-knowledge and revitalizing the human spirit" to which Nell, Drew, and Bush refer.

Contemplative Self Active Play in Palliative Care

Terri Drew is currently a Nurse Practitioner for the Veterans Health Ad-ministration in San Francisco-Santa Rosa, California, where she pro-vides helpful medical, mental, and palliative care consultations with patients and families experiencing complicated and/or traumatic life changes. Her previous work as an acute care provider and nurse ed-ucator have informed the following case studies, as she continues to seek positive psychology approaches to care. In her writing, we see how Contemplative Self Active Play *is used as an integrative practice in meeting persons where they are for the facilitation of self-actualization and wellbeing.*

The Center to Advance Palliative Care (CAPC) responds to persons' symptoms associated with chronic or life limiting illness by sup-porting patient-centered wishes for care in aging and end of life. The initiated document of Precepts for Palliative Care, published by the Task Force for Palliative Care in 1997, sought to align health care with patient wishes through conversations that promote un-derstanding of desired goals for care, dignity and quality of life.

According to a testimony of many healthcare clinicians and the Hospice and Palliative Nurses Association (HPNA) call for research in 2012-2015 (HPNA, 2012), palliative care clinicians have tools to assess the presence of persons' psychological distress including physical pain, anxiety and depression, but lack strategies to miti-gate these disturbances (HPNA, 2012). We have since seen advances in interdisciplinary and pharmaceutical symptom management that significantly improve quality of life, yet approaches to support self-insight to meaningfulness of experience, redefined hope and self-actualization (as discussed by Maslow in his works), may yet benefit by the use of play. Play is readily applied in mainstream child development, yet far less so in aging. Play has been largely untapped as a resource for palliative care consultations with older adults who experience developmental life challenges, yet as discussed in the forthcoming case studies, is shown to offer an effective approach to building resilience and perceptually expanded consciousness of health (Newman, 2007).

When children have the opportunity to construct and reconstruct emotional, physical and spiritual themes in play, they form new neuropathways, or riverbeds of thought processes that potentiate neuroplasticity and resilience. Resilience is a crucial intrinsic resource associated with improved perceptions of self-efficacy, and as such is a profound determinant in wellbeing and positive health outcomes (Bandura, 1997). Relative to palliative care consultations, when addressing complex challenges, goals for care and quality of life, the use of open-ended materials in *Contemplative Self Active Play* may potentiate a person's capacity to form new associations, and abstract into relevant internal meaning. Play also engages a person's intrinsic coping skills and organic up-regulation of positive endorphins such as dopamine and serotonin: neurochemicals crucial to wellbeing and perceptions of self-efficacy.

Contemplative Self Active Play in older adult settings has been observed in the two cases presented, as a non-pharmaceutical palliative care approach for the facilitation of insight to values and cultural meaning, symptom management, and the fostering of effective therapeutic relationships. Through the use of wood blocks, paints, and other open-ended materials, volunteer participants discussed themes that surfaced within their play milieu. Participants explored different possibilities in building, restructuring, evoking memory, new discovery and alternate perceptions of constructs that support resilience. The mechanism of this intervention may be understood as analogous to Piaget's developmental stages, seen in highly resilient periods from childhood to adolescence, in concrete to abstract thinking, from simple concepts to a greater under-standing of the connection between intrinsic and environmental influences. Older adults and caregivers are observed benefitting from the opportunity to engage in an evolution of creative purpose and self-efficacy that may further promote beneficial palliative care relationships.

The following abbreviated case studies illustrate the clinical application of *Contemplative Self Active Play*. The first case study took place in a Medical-Surgical Unit at a community hospital. The second was conducted at a clinical nursing program in a long-term care facility (LTC). Both case studies incorporated the *Contemplative Self Active Play* process as a palliative intervention involving spontaneous creative engagement that drew upon prior life experience and renewed insight, as constructed during the play experience.

Case One: During a stay at a community hospital on a medical-surgical unit in Bakersfield, CA, a 78 year-old woman was hospitalized with an acute chronic obstructive pulmonary disease (COPD) exacerbation and anxiety. Roberta is the mother of a 36 year-old disabled daughter dependent on her for support. Roberta's husband required chemotherapy treatment. Roberta was overwhelmed with her present medical situation:

> *"How can I care for my daughter, my husband? This is my first hospital admission. It's never been this bad."*

The facilitator of the palliative care consultation provided to Roberta, a set of 36 Dr. Drew's Blocks (2 x 3 x 1/2 inch) and two blue wooden circles (4 x 1 inch). They sat with one another and discussed goals for care, and the challenges Roberta experienced. Roberta held the wooden blocks in her hand and began to build a square box. She stated:

> *"That's me, a walled in box when I can't breathe, no way out and no solution."*

The facilitator mostly listened and asked a few questions, as Roberta began to restructure the square into a pyramid, changing out blocks, rebalancing the structure, placing the circles in different poses. As she moved the blocks to fit the structure and goals she wished to build, Roberta began to have the experience of surfacing insight and she vocalized new possibilities for additional care that she had previously overlooked. When she completed the activity, Roberta referred to having redefined hope with possible resources for the challenge she was facing, she noted she felt calmer. Roberta's experience during a 20-minute *Contemplative Self Active Play* session addressed two components to well-being, "openness to experience, and the discovery of [one's] emotional intelligence" (Carmody and Baer 2008. pg. 24).

Case Two: Nursing students participated as researchers in a palliative care quality of life intervention to address physical, emotional, cognitive, social and spiritual health of volunteers, within a long-term care facility in Morro Bay, CA. The nursing students asked residents if they would like to volunteer to participate in a 30-minute *Contemplative Self Active Play* (CSAP) activity an hour after lunch, in one of the facility's activity rooms. Open-ended materials, including blocks, paint, white paper and brushes were provided. Nursing students were briefed on palliative communication concepts. Data was collected by photo action research, and included journal statements made by resident volunteers. The nursing students acted as researchers and observers of their own experience.

Following the CSAP activity, benefits noted by the LTC nursing staff were, two of five participants, who typically requested an opioid for pain, or a benzodiazepine for anxiety, did not ask for their afternoon dose. They also noted mood improvements. Themes noted by students were enhanced experience of relationship building and increased cultural awareness of the diversity and complexity of aging. One nursing student stated:

> *"I saw another side of 'Gloria', not just a patient with multiple symptoms. At first, she said she couldn't participate, she was in too much pain, then with encouragement, she decided to paint with a brush and watercolors. At the end she was smiling, she didn't even ask for her pain medication!"*

Another nursing student stated:

"I didn't know Dell grew up on an Indian Reservation and had a different response than I assumed about how medication worked."

Another nursing student stated:

"My resident has a history of depression and anxiety with tendency to isolate, doesn't join in activities like bingo and movie day, stays in bed, but she agreed to join me today. At the end, she was sitting at a table with others and asked, 'When are we going to do this again?' "

Another nursing student responded:

"I learned my resident founded the Epilepsy Society; she said she gave lectures across the country when many people still thought it meant being possessed by the devil. She told me she hasn't been eating because she's grieving about her first love who had inspired her to do her work, he passed away last week."

The nursing students noted that the residents' narrations provided insight into goals for care, such as the cause of nutritional decline of one participant. Common themes expressed were a deeper connection with care recipients and meaning that led to discovered application for goals of care, and alternative approaches to pain and symptom management.

Photographs and journal writings from volunteer participants revealed older adults reflecting on who they were in the context of life experience, health care challenges and community resources. Providers of palliative care when utilizing *Contemplative Self Active Play* may enhance their knowledge of care recipients' values, culture and meaningfulness, thus enhancing patient-centered and team-based palliative care delivery.

Health First: *Applying Self Active Play with Grieving Children and Families*

Illness and death are a part of life and so is the grief process that allows one to move toward hope, healing, and renewal. For a child who has lost a loved one, the road to healing can be filled with silent pain and grief. Commonly called "silent grievers," children deal with the loss of a loved one in a unique way, and their path toward healing is difficult and different from adults. Self active play is being used as an intervention tool that strengthens resiliency and enables children to process their trauma and grief to better cope with their loss.

In 2012, the staff and volunteers of the Bright Star Center for Grieving Children and Families, a Hospice Program of Health First in Melbourne, Florida, was introduced to the principles of self active play and play protocols. In mixed-age groups of children and families, self active play was introduced as a training component for staff and volunteers working at the grief center.

The Bright Star Center directors, Cynthia Koppler and Terry Musso, realized the value of self active play and were instrumental in the creation and implementation of this intervention. The client population is primarily middle-class families of various ethnicities. These families have experienced the full spectrum of loss, such as loss of a child, spouse, sibling or grandparent. These deaths may have been from illness, accident, violent death or suicide.

The primary objective of the play training was to help parents and their grieving children value and use play as a resource for emotional wellness. The idea was for parents to realize that self active play builds self-efficacy and reinforces a sense of control by promoting creativity, optimism and resiliency to better cope with challenging life transitions.

Observations During the Self Active Play Intervention

Each child in the Bright Star program spent one of their grief group sessions engaged in self active play. The children had freedom to choose their own materials. Using these materials encouraged the children to focus, explore, organize, imagine and create without feeling obligated to produce a product or complete a pre-described task.

Each child displayed a distinctive way of working with the materials. These included:

- *stacking objects and striving to build as high as possible.*

- *arranging objects in spirals*

- *creating environments—buildings, towns, homes*

- *spelling out names of loved ones*

- *fanciful creations that appeared to exist just as spontaneous arrangements*

- *representations of useful vehicles such as a spaceship, cars and boats*

Children initiated action and were proactive in their engagements with the objects. Some of the children spent their entire time making just one thing and sitting back to admire it. Other children would build, tear down, and rebuild something completely different. The children were initiating and gaining control over their play circumstances.

Through this process, themes emerged from the observations and debriefing sessions with the children and parents. These themes included:

- *experience of joy*

- *sense of accomplishment and pride*

- *establishment of control over external materials*

Each of these themes are significant when working with children suffering from traumatic loss. Grieving children frequently struggle with a sense of powerlessness after the death of a loved one. Communication breaks down and all but disappears. Children lose interest in school and their world in general. Self active play helps to reverse that tendency given play stimulates creative energy and optimism. More often it is the pure enjoyment of play and communication that brings them to a place of joy and healing. It allows children to look forward to life, albeit altered due to the loss of a loved one. The aim of supporting children and their families after a loss is to help the family, and the child specifically, to go on living with the expectation that there will be exciting, challenging and joyful times ahead.

Experience and Reflection of Parents

The parents also needed time to play as did the children. As a result, there was a play experience designed for just the parents. During the parent's play they were able to connect with deep thoughts and feelings. As we observed with the children, several themes emerged following the parents' play experience:

- *joy of play and shared joy with other parents*

- *recognition of the ability to create something unique*

- *feelings of accomplishment and pride*

In the following excerpts from the parents' reflective journals, we see how parents used the play experience to process their grief and communicate personal revelations. Parent insights impacted how they relate with their children, their children's grief, and other members of the family.

- *I wanted to string the beads together at first but didn't have any string. So,...I just placed the beads where I wanted to spell my angel's name. At first I thought I might just make a pattern with the beads but then I thought to spell her name. I cried because it just makes me think of her and I miss her. It also reminded me of the Beads of Courage that she earned during her treatment. She got different beads for every different treatment she had. She got red beads for each blood transfusion; white for each time she got chemo, yellow for each night she spent in the hospital, etc. She earned a butterfly bead when she died to earn her butterfly/angel wings. Then I used the remaining beads to form a heart to signify my love for her.*

The play experience was a way of relating and expressing the meaning and the pain associated with her daughter's fight against cancer. Beads became the medium to represent the different phases

of her daughter's fight. Healing occurs as this mother opens up and shares her expression of her suffering.

Another parent shared her own experience using the objects to express her insight and fight with cancer:

- *I recreated the tumors growing in my liver. From black corks to blood red corks to copper metal, interspersed with clear tops representing healthy tissue. I found out this morning that my chemo is no longer working. This activity was very helpful to me to visualize my cancer. There is meaning here and understanding that which cannot be understood. Children need that also. There is so much they do not understand and need to learn by themselves.*

In the following journal the play provided a positive way of controlling and expressing the deep, emotional, inner feelings. Without provocation this parent wrote:

- *I chose the shiny round caps because they were on a blue blanket and I love the colors blue and silver. I made a heart for the love I have for my husband and that is also why I made his initials M. J. P. I also made a smiley face because that is how my son and I feel today. We are going on vacation and are excited about it. I really miss my husband. Yesterday was his 7-month anniversary of his death. Ten years ago we were planning our wedding. On our tenth anniversary we were supposed to renew our wedding vows. Saturday will be bittersweet for me which is why my son and I are going on vacation. My son is a clone of his father and I am truly blessed to have him in my life.*

After the parents finished their play, they were invited to come see what the children had made during their play. The parents were amazed as they listened to their children describe their play. In some cases, the parents began playing with their children. As mentioned earlier, following traumatic events there is a breakdown of communication, a type of psychological distancing or disengagement that happens between family members. The fact that parents willingly joined in the play with their children indicates a healing and strengthening of the relationship between the child and adult as they play. The parents who actively played with their children saw the most value of using play to help grieving families.

The following parent responses describe what it was like listening to their child represent their play.

- *Interesting to see how she involved some of her real life into her fantasy creative play.*

- *It made my heart happy. It's really hard to watch my child struggle with her grief. My daughter has a great imagination, is creative but also shy. I thoroughly enjoyed listening and watching her play.*

- *Very enlightening to have an opening into my son's train of thought. He draws very often and I usually inquire about what he was thinking about. His response almost always brings a smile and warms my heart.*

- *I was very proud that she was able to tell me and everyone about what she had created. Normally she is very shy and unable to tell a story.*

- *I was amazed my oldest is usually very quiet but with this she was ready to express. My middle daughter didn't surprise me. She has a very descriptive imagination. My youngest usually is loud but was very quiet and engaged.*

The parents recognized and valued the joy and creativity that their children were experiencing in their play. Parents were then asked if there was anything about what the children shared that surprised them. These are the comments the parents shared:

- *As disorganized and flighty as my daughter seems to be on certain tasks, I was surprised that her building was completely symmetrical. I was also surprised that she volunteered to talk in front of the group.*

- *I was surprised my son enjoyed it as much. With him being older he's usually into video games, tv, computer and I have to force him to do creative things. But here he seemed really into it.*

Parents recognized the connection between the play and real life. For a grieving family it is not easy to play together. Grief is in the way of communicating and relating to one another. Play, if one can get to it, serves as an antidote to pain and suffering. The final question that the parents were asked was what was it like for you to play and create with your child:

- *Fun and less stressful time to interact with her.*

- *I love the way we made a plan of what we were going to build together. We need to do this more often. Thank you.*

- *Totally fun!*

- *Great bonding experience.*

- *Fantastic to let them take the lead and me not giving direction. That there was no arguing between them. We worked together.*

- *It helps me feel closer to him. A great bonding experience for me. Lovely to enjoy his company while he is doing something he loves so much.*

The play provided family units with time away from the grief. The play creates a distraction from the distress associated with grieving.

CONCLUSION

THIS CHAPTER SHARED how self active play provides relief from the suffering. While appropriate for early childhood classroom practice, self active play is a positive way of helping those suffering from abuse, medical concerns, or sudden traumatic loss. The four dramatic studies in this chapter show how self active play provides relief for children and adults. Often overlooked and undervalued in our culture, play is a source of healing and creative power. Self active play is a positive "time out" from the heavy burden that many of these children and adults carried in the Bright Star case study and for the children from Transylvania. We also saw how self active play is successfully applied in palliative care and the training of nurses.

Chapter 7

Advocacy and Resilience

"Play serves the serious purpose of education, but the player is not deliberately educating himself or herself. The player is playing for fun; education is a by-product. If the player were playing for a serious purpose, it would no longer be play and much of the educative power would be lost."

—Peter Gray, (2013, p. 154)

IN THIS CHAPTER we suggest an infrastructure for play advocacy. *Advocacy* is defined as "the act of pleading for, supporting, or recommending" (Dictionary.com, 2018). In previous chapters we have clearly defined self-active play and shown examples of how it has benefitted children and adults. It is clear from the American Academy of Pediatrics Report that toxic stress has detrimental and long-lasting effects in the lives of children. Self-active play is an antidote to the harmful consequences of play deprivation. We have shown that children suffer when they are denied the freedom to play as a means of satisfying a basic human need to explore, create, and otherwise develop and reach their potential. The evidence is very clear and confirming that play is about brain and heart development.

Our book, *Self Active Play*, offers a proven way of addressing, educating, and positively impacting the lives of children and adults. Through self-active play children realize their capacity to be creative and overcome impediments to happy learning. Play opportunities can reduce children's suffering. Being a strong, effective advocate for self-active play means providing children play opportunities that alleviate stress, anxiety and suffering. Our research suggests that play education and the self-active play process reduces suffering for adults as well, as a means for self-reflection, inner understanding, and regaining resilience.

The relationship between play and resilience is especially important. *Resilience* is the "ability to recover readily from illness, depression, adversity, or the like; buoyancy" (Dictionary.com, 2018). Milteer and Ginsburg state, "Play is a natural tool that children can and should use to build their resilience. At its core, the development of resilience is about learning to overcome challenges and adversity" (p. 205, 2012). They further argue that play allows children a safe context in which to face their fears, try new options in meeting those fears, and persevere through the problem solving to the solution. Through fantasy play children are able to develop scenarios that provide them with opportunities to face their fears and then create ways of overcoming those fears. Therefore, we aim to help educate about, build, and reinforce a play culture that recognizes, respects, and promotes self-active play in the lives of children and adults.

Resilience

Dr. Glen Richardson developed a working model to understand resilience. According to him, "A succinct statement of resilience theory is that there is a force within everyone that drives them to seek self-actualization, altruism, wisdom, and harmony with a spiritual source of strength. This force is resilience" (2002, 313). His work outlined the waves of research that have underpinned resiliency research. The first wave of research identified resilient qualities in the individual, such as self-esteem, self-efficacy, and support systems in place for that individual. The second wave of research investigated the process of resiliency, identifying various stressors, adversities, changes, and opportunities for the development of protective factors. Protective factors were defined as qualities that enable the individual to bounce back or overcome adversity but also serve as a way of coping when the next disturbance occurs. The self-active play process is a means for coping with disturbances.

(Reprinted with permission, Dr. G. E. Richardson)

According to Richardson's model, people have four ways of dealing with life stressors, or disruptors. First, they can simply ignore the life disruptors and remain in a state of homeostasis, unmoved by the disturbance. We can think of this reaction as the metaphor of an ostrich with its head buried in the sand. The second response to disturbances is to deal with it through what Richardson calls reintegration by loss. This type of response includes the person giving up some sort of motivation, hope, or drive in order to return to homeostasis. The third response is a negative way, dysfunctional reintegration. This includes, for example, using alcohol or drugs to achieve a state of homeostasis. The final, most productive response to disturbances is resilient reintegration. In this process of personal growth, the experience provides the individual with the opportunity to fully understand the disturbance, identify components of the disturbance, and create ways of working through the disturbance. This process allows the individual to grow and, more importantly, develop protective factors that will support them when they face another disturbance in the future. Self-active play is an advocacy tool for promoting resilient reintegration. As Gray notes, "Play is nature's way of teaching children how to solve their own problems, control their impulses, modulate their emotions, see from others' perspectives, negotiate differences, and get along with others as equals." Gray (2013, 175).

There is danger in living life without a repertoire of healthy coping and problem-solving strategies. Ignoring or sugarcoating a problem won't produce self-supportive strategies to face disturbances in positive ways that stimulate personal growth. Self-active play promotes creative ways of thinking and wondering and generates innovative possibilities. It provides a context in which multiple strategies can be tested for potential use in the future, whether players are young or old.

Social Resilience

Up until this point we've considered self-active play as a process that affects individuals on multiple levels and in multiple ways. We now want to consider how self-active play may promote resilient changes beyond the individual level by examining the cumulative impact of self-active play on communities or social groups. This is known as social resilience. We first learned of it in Mark Drew's work with marine ecological systems, but the concept originated in the early 1970s, when Dr. C. Stanley Holling examined it from an ecological perspective. His interpretation of the term *social resilience* referred to how adaptive a species was to environmental factors that affected its ability to survive and thrive—in other words, how well the species was able to cope with disturbances in its environment and then bounce back to its basic state (Trkulja, 2015).

Social resilience became a popular concept and soon appeared in multiple fields of study. Work done by Adger (2000) suggested that social resilience was defined as the ability of groups or communities to cope with external stresses and disturbances as a result of social, political, or environmental change. Folke (2016) suggested that social resilience consisted of four basic features: *adaptability, relationships, diversity, and creativity.* Adaptability is an understanding that life is full of surprises and unknowns. Acceptance of uncertainty as a part of life can then be used as an opportunity for social change. The relationships feature accepts and celebrates the connections between members. It is through these relationships that social groups are able to respond in positive and agile ways to inevitable changes. Diversity, which is closely related to the relationships feature, recognizes the importance of the individual knowledge base that each member brings to the social group. Creativity recognizes the forming of divergent thinking, which in turn adds support for building social resilience.

All of the features that Folke identified can be easily tied to the benefits of self-active play. In the previous chapters we outlined and documented how self-active play provides players with the ability to think in flexible ways as they manipulate objects and consider potential uses for them; thus, it promotes adaptability. Players recognize connections between the objects and their own movements when manipulating the objects and thus appreciate relationships. Players also appreciate the individual characteristics of the play materials that provide diversity. Finally, self-active play is a catapult for creativity, for stimulating divergent thinking, wonder, and imagination. These qualities, which we normally attribute to individuals, also apply to a group or culture.

Self-active play supports the growth and development of the individual player. It also provides a context for individuals to form small social groups with a common thread, and a belief in the importance of play for the health and well-being of both individuals and their social group. These social groups share common attitudes and beliefs about the importance of play and support each other as they work to change the cultural perspectives of others. In order to build a play culture, in which play is held in high esteem as an expected experience for all children and adults, there needs to be a major shift. We believe that, through self-active play experiences, individuals, small groups, and the larger culture can respond in resilient ways to change attitudes and beliefs about the importance of play in the lives of children and adults.

Resilience and the Principles of Self-Active Play

When we connect the principles of self-active play, discussed in chapter 2, with the concept of resilience, there is clear alignment between the two. Milteer and Ginsburg state that play is a safe context in which children can rehearse adult roles and try out different possibilities. (p. 206). This statement is directly connected to Self Active Play *Principle 1*, *Principle 2*, and *Principle 3* regarding creative energy flowing, spontaneously balancing and strengthening hope, will, and creates a state of being where you feel safer, more trusting, and capable. Self-active play releases creative energy, which in turn enables the child to imagine possibilities to explore. During these times of query, children investigate possible responses to questions or situations they face in this imaginary world and also situations they may be facing in the real world. By trying new possibilities in play, children acquire new options that they may also use in real life. And so it is with adults.

Principle 4 and *Principle 5* describe play as a state of being where exploration is encouraged and the creative energy allows us to imagine, to pretend new roles of power as we discover who we are and what we are capable of doing or being. The play experience develops resilience through the creative energy and the desire to return to the play space. Resilience is indeed a possible outcome of play experiences. Play provides an avenue on which to build a clearer understanding of our capacities and the new possibilities. In the moving of the objects, the ordering and reordering, we realize our lives require us to utilize the same process so that we can readjust, make meaning out of chaos, thus be resilient. Self-active play also develops self-awareness, providing children with ways to identify and understand their own abilities, likes, wants, and needs. And so it is with adults.

Principle 6 states, in part, that the feelings generated during a play experience "are not isolated to the play space but rather move forward as the player moves beyond the play space in their realities." This principle depicts one of the major intersections between play and resiliency, the ability of the player to use ideas, emotions, and problem-solving strategies that were developed and created during play in their own realities. This has been seen in play therapy research when children express their feelings through their play. And so it is with adults.

Finally, *Principle 7* speaks of building a trust in one's intuitive self. Self-active play is an avenue to the creation of a sense of competence, accomplishment, and expertise. Self-active play strategies develop problem solving and self-determination and thus create a self-image on which the child can stand firmly. Knowing one's own preferences and then connecting those preferences to confidence produces a competent, productive, and caring individual. This is resilience, the capacity to overcome adversity, a toughness to persevere. And so it is with adults.

There is always another problem. The more ways children learn how to deal with problems, the better off they will be. Play is a safe space in which to address and solve problems. In play, children and adults alike realize they can identify and solve problems as they build and work with one another in ways they enjoy and feel good about the process. This authentic play originates from deep within the player, even though there is interaction with the external world.

Open-ended materials, which are key to self-active play, also help build resilience: in playing with the materials, the unexpected always happens and players learn how to deal with it. Players get better at solving problems, evaluating tangible structural integrity and physical elements and arranging the materials. Players decide where to put the next block, cap, or cylinder to serve an idea. Players assume an influential position and express intent with these simple tools just to see how it turns out. Along the way, difficulty, uncertainty, ambiguity, and problems arise, and players must figure out a comfortable solution, one that they and perhaps other people appreciate. Young social beings, members of a community, engage in the construction of knowledge through play. Delight grows. This is good for young children, and, we say again, so it is with adults.

Becoming a Self-Active Play Advocate

Advocacy begins with a strong sense of calling, believing passionately for instance in the importance of play. Strong advocacy movements begin with passionate individuals who then connect with other like minded individuals into small groups. Several community organizations already exist that believe in the power of play, such as the National Association for the Education of Young Children (NAEYC), or The Association for the Study of Play (TASP) or the Institute for Self Active Education (ISAE). These organizations bring individuals together to research play and promote advocacy.

For example, NAEYC has gone through an organizational change and now states can create their own "statewide play chapters" that are linked to the Play, Policy and Practice Interest Forum, a source of support for play advocacy. TASP is an organization devoted to the intense study and practice of play from multiple disciplines, such as psychology, sociology, and biology. ISAE studies and promotes self active play experiences with children and adults in diverse contexts.

The Story: *The Finnish Perspective*

Finland is an interesting example of national advocacy for a system-wide educational reform that emphasizes play across the curriculum in theory and in practice within the schools.

As a result, in 2000, Finland found itself in the international limelight after outscoring all other countries on the Programme for International Student Assessment (PISA) test in reading, math, and science. This was a surprise to the world in general but also to Finland. How or why had Finland outscored all other nations? Most authorities considered that year's test results a fluke, an improbable feat that would not be repeated. But those pesky Finns went and did it again, and the country has ranked among the top in PISA test scores ever since.

Finland's educational system believes and practices the idea that children should take part in unstructured time for play, which is well documented in research in child development. Furthermore, incorporating play as an integral part of children's education is part of the culture of the school, which is supported by families, local authorities, the Finnish National Agency for Education, and the Ministry of Education. Therefore, Finland is an important example of how when children's well being is the primary focus of education, then the results of that effort are manifested in multiple ways, including more competent, resilient children and higher test scores. In the case of Finland a whole nation has advocated and made a commitment to what is good for children and teachers, this includes play.

Finland has built an exceptional educational system that is fundamentally different in several ways from the standardized testing of the United States and other countries. Pasi Sahlberg, a leading authority on the Finnish educational system, notes in his 2015 book, *Finnish Lessons 2.0: What Can the World Learn from Educational Change in Finland?*, "The Finnish recipe for good education is simple: Always ask yourself if the policy or reform you plan to initiate is going to be good for children or teachers" (xxiii). Sahlberg was educated in Finnish schools and became a teacher himself, then moved on to the university to teach teacher preparation. He holds a high degree of credibility when he states that the educational reforms in Finland are based on trust in teachers and their professional integrity. He goes on to state that establishing a system of reform based on trusting the teachers allows for more local teaching autonomy. In Finland, teaching has become the number-one choice of vocation among young people. Teachers are well prepared for their professional obligations to children through university teacher-preparation programs and are trusted to use that expertise. The Finnish system gives hope to other educational systems that public education can work for all children. Sahlberg notes that this kind of educational transformation takes "time, patience and determination" (7).

In a 2017 book, *Empowered Educators in Finland: How High-Performing Systems Shape Teacher Quality*, Sahlberg and coauthors Karen Hammerness, Raisa Ahtiainen noted that a lesson in Finland lasts approximately forty-five minutes, leaving fifteen minutes for recess; this means that in a typical day, schoolchildren in Finland have over ninety minutes of recess (43). The Basic Education Decree of 1998 states its appreciation for "the necessity of healthy breaks between cognitive work for children as well as the importance of social interaction and learning through play" (Basic Education Decree 1998, 852).

Another interesting fact cited by Hammerness, Ahtianinen, and Sahlberg is that Finland is using research and documentation from the United States to support their views on the importance of play in the lives of young children. They cite the American Academy of Pediatrics 2011 report by Milteer and Ginsburg that supports play as a means for promoting health and well-being for children and their families. We need to become stronger advocates and work together to pursue this heartfelt truth. We also need to keep in mind that this kind of systemic change takes time, conversation, and diligence; and it must be centered on what is good for children and teachers.

Preparing Future Teachers for Play Advocacy

Michael Patte, a Professor of Teaching and Learning from Bloomsburg University in Pennsylvania shares a vibrant example of how a community of play advocates worked together to share their passion for play. Dr. Patte was a co-presenter of Hands On Play Experiences along with ISAE for a number of years at the NAEYC National Conference. Dr. Patte shares his journey as a play advocate in the story below.

Even though my days as an early childhood and elementary school teacher have long since passed, I continue to advocate, think, and write about the importance of play in the lives of children. I have been a teacher educator for the past fifteen years at Bloomsburg University in Pennsylvania. BU has a rich and storied history in the art and science of teacher preparation, having been founded as a "normal school" in 1869. In the early part of the twentieth century many normal schools like BU offered a program called The Normal Course in Play—Materials for Use in the Training of Playground and Recreation Workers (NCIP), created by the Playground Association of America (1925). The main purpose for establishing the program was "to make community recreation vital and to give the spirit of play value as a philosophy for life" (PRAA 1925, v). The NCIP was multidisciplinary in nature and broad in scope. Curricular topics included program planning, the nature and function of play, play leadership, play facilities, organization and administration, and history of the community recreation movement.

Flash forward nearly one hundred years to 2018, and the Normal Course in Play and its core purposes have all but vanished from teacher education training programs across America. As an illustrative example, today, BU students with a major of early childhood education (PK–4) must successfully complete a minimum of forty (three-credit) classes with only one focusing on play (Fine Arts and Expressive Play for the Developing Child). I am often assigned to teach the course due in part to my content-level expertise along with fifteen years of practical teaching experience, first in preschool and then in fifth grade. My teaching experience in preschool was joyous and playful, while fifth grade was serious and academic. A real-world problem that I witness each day as a fieldwork supervisor of student teachers is academic classroom environments devoid of play.

Current research along with my practical experience suggests that teachers new to the profession enter schools that are indifferent to children's play. Therefore, it is necessary to equip preservice teacher candidates with a comprehensive toolbox of dispositions, skills, and strategies to promote play both inside and outside of the school classroom. I fill up the metaphorical toolboxes in the Fine

Arts and Expressive Play for the Developing Child course by exploring the role of the fine arts and play on whole-child development, creating opportunities for participation in the fine arts and play across multiple settings, developing skills to enhance the play lives of children, exploring methods for integrating the fine arts and play into the curriculum, and developing the skills to advocate for the fine arts and play as an essential element to childhood.

Although many of the preservice teacher candidates attending BU believe that opportunities for play at school should be readily available, those teacher candidates often feel powerless to enact change if those opportunities are not present. Therefore, developing, refining, and actualizing advocacy skills becomes a major focus of the course. One course assignment is a fine arts/play advocacy project that requires students to investigate a timely topic related to the fine arts and play explored throughout the semester and then develop an individual advocacy project to be shared publicly via a demonstration, elevator speech, letter to the editor, or similar communication.

Pop-Up Playground

In the fall of 2017 students enrolled in the Fine Arts and Expressive Play for the Developing Child course decided to organize, publicize, and implement a community play day advocacy project to support opportunities for self-directed, child-initiated play for children and families. The Pop-Up Playground concept is the brainchild of two playworkers from the United Kingdom, Morgan Leichter-Saxby and Suzanna Law, whose sole mission is to support children's right to play in schools, neighborhoods, museums, parks, and anywhere children reside. Their website (popupadventureplaygrounds.wordpress.com) provides a variety of free resources (including a toolkit, resource pack, and benefits of play flyer) to help facilitate a successful Pop-Up Playground. Simply defined, Pop-Up Playgrounds are one-day events that provide opportunities for child-initiated play in public settings using a wide variety of common, everyday loose parts. These loose parts include safe, clean, open-ended materials including recyclable items (cardboard boxes, plastic bottles, tires, tubes), everyday things (tape, string, yarn, play dough), household wares (pots, pans, bowls, wooden spoons), natural materials (branches, leaves, pine cones), and other things (fabric, old telephones, computer keyboards).

There are seven guiding principles for running a Pop-Up Playground spelled out in the Resource Pack (Leicher-Saxby, Juster, & Law 2012). First, children are free to attend as there is never a charge to participate. Second, children and their families are free to come and go as they please. All participants arrive and leave at their own discretion. Third, children participate at the Pop-Up as they wish, making their own choices and directing their own actions. Fourth, Pop-Ups are inclusive and open to people of all genders, backgrounds, abilities, and interests. Fifth, all of the materials explored at a Pop-Up are common everyday objects and things. Sixth, Pop-Ups are free from hazards and provide children with a safe play space to assess and manage risk. Finally, Pop-Ups are commercial-free zones where no products are sold; it's all about children's play.

The Bloomsburg University Pop-Up Playground was held on Saturday, November 11, from 11:00 a.m. to 4:00 p.m. in the Student Recreation Center. The event was entirely staffed by BU students, and all of the loose parts, food, and T-shirts were donated. Close to four hundred children and family members from the surrounding community attended the BU Pop-Up event. By all accounts the event was a huge success. When asked to report what they enjoyed most about the BU Pop-Up event, family members reported "opportunities for creative play in a new environment," "that the children were given endless supplies to create without instruction," "not worrying about something breaking," "encouraging the use of imagination," "the atmosphere where children can freely play without limits on material usage or a requirement to clean up," and "the freedom for children to do what they wanted."

We also asked the preservice teacher candidates who facilitated the BU Pop-Up Playground to share a highlight of their overall experience. One student shared, "My biggest highlight was being able to walk around and see all of the children's imaginations at work. All of the children's creations were unique in their own way. I like that the parents did not interfere or try to direct the play." A second student enjoyed "seeing the pure joy on the faces of the children. It isn't every day that children get the chance to use their imagination and a seemingly unending supply of material to create their own dream in the form of cardboard boxes." An additional student's biggest highlight was "seeing the parents play with their children. A lot of parents work long hours every day and may not have much time to play with their children. The Pop-Up event provided the time to create something together out of common objects. It was beautiful to experience."

Now, more than any time in the recent past, we must prepare the next generation of teachers to advocate for the child's right to play at home, at school, and in the community. As the field of education forges into the twenty-first century it should not forget the important lessons and traditions learned from the past. We must once again advocate "to make community recreation vital and to give the spirit of play value as a philosophy for life" (PRAA 1925, v).

Play & Prosperity

Michael Wragg, Senior Lecturer at Leeds Beckett University, School of Health and Community Studies in the United Kingdom, describes the consequences of the deficit of play and the future employment prospects of individuals. Having a playful mindset in the workplace strengthens your passion for your work. Having the view that play and work are not diametrically opposed states of being, are compatible, and necessary to the healthy adult.

It is well documented in the literature that for children growing up in the United States, United Kingdom, and much of the developed world, opportunities to play freely have, over the course of the last two generations, decreased markedly (Gray 2011). Consequences of an absence of free play for children's development have been theorized, researched, and analyzed in the literature for some time. Stated concerns regarding the consequence of a play deficit have typically tended to concentrate on its negative impact on children's health. Physical and mental; anxiety, stress, obesity, and depression are all associated with a decrease in children's freedom to play (Butland, Jebb, Kopelman, 2007).

Emerging concern regarding play deprivation is the effect of limited play on children future employment prospects. Stuart Brown, in his 2009 publication *Play: How it Shapes the Brain, Opens the Imagination and Invigorates the Soul*, discusses two consultants, Frank Wilson, a neurologist and author of the book *The Hand: How its Use Shapes the Brain, Language and Human Culture*, and Nate Johnson, a mechanics teacher in a high school in Long Beach, who found that his students were increasingly less competent than previous cohorts at solving problems. In his endeavors to discover why, Johnson concluded that it was because they hadn't played enough with their hands in childhood. Johnson and Wilson collaborated to work for NASA and Boeing as consultants designing play programs to improve the problem-solving capabilities of newly recruited research and development problem solvers (Brown 2009).

Problem solving is one example of a number of "soft" employment skills, the development of which are strongly associated with play. These "soft" skills have been found, by surveys of business leaders and employers, to be lacking in today's graduates. A study by McKinsey, cited in Mourshed, Farrell, & Barton. (2012), found that 45 percent of US employers cited the main reason for entry-level job vacancies as a lack of such skills in graduates. The same study found that only 42 percent of employers worldwide believe new gradu-ates are adequately prepared for work, and a 2014 study by Career-Builder found that 40 percent of employers believe students lack problem solving skills, 39 percent aren't sufficiently creative in their thinking, and 37 percent have inadequate oral communication (Ca-reerBuilder 2014). Similarly, a 2016 report by the World Economic Forum found that employees' cognitive abilities, including creativ-ity and logical reasoning; social skills, namely negotiation, persua-sion and emotional intelligence; and process skills, encompassing active listening and critical thinking, are both running at a critical shortage and growing in demand.

These shortages and deficiencies might be explained by a lack of play in children's lives. One factor compromising children's freedom to play is the pursuance of overly-academicized educa-tion practices. The United States and United Kingdom continue to follow an education policy that emphasizes didactic teaching and learning methods which have ranked top of international compar-ative tables for pupil performance, particularly in math and sci-ence. In South Korea it has been documented that the country's best graduates aren't suited to the jobs being offered, while in Chi-na, the phrase *goafen dineng,* meaning "good at tests, but bad at ev-erything else," has become used commonly to describe its school pupils (Klein 2013). Evidence suggests their graduates don't possess the skills demanded by the new global economy so the education-al system has reduced academic burdens, de-emphasized the im-portance of test results, and provided more time for free play and self-initiated activity in the school day (Zhao 2015).

Play is well established in the literature as a process central to developing the types of cognitive and social employability skills, which, according to Universities UK/CBI (2009) and the World Economic Forum (2016) are most highly prized by employers. Play promotes flexible thinking and facilitates the acquisition of person-al resources that can be drawn on in times of need (Frederickson, 2006); the enjoyment of playing has benefits for problem solving and enhances performance (Isen & Reeve 2006; Pressman & Cohen 2005); there is a positive relationship between cognitive skills and high quality play (Gmitrova & Gmitrov 2004), and play is linked to creativity in the sense that it involves divergent thinking, symbol substitution, positive affect—a term used to describe the extent to which an individual subjectively experiences positive moods such as joy, interest, and alertness (Rhyff and Singer 1998)—problem solving skills, and emotion regulation (Russ, 2003).

Education specialists and business leaders are increasingly coming to regard traditional, formally instructive teaching practices as a hindrance to global economic progress (WEF 2016). The continued dominance of this approach to children's education is attributed to an outmoded legacy of the twentieth century. Due to the unprecedented pace of change in the twenty first century global labor market, accelerated by the rapid evolution of artificial intelligence, 3-D printing, biotechnology, robotics, and smart systems, it is predicted that 65 percent of children entering first grade today will find themselves working in job types that don't yet exist (Fisch & McLeod 2017). The outdated educational system seems increasingly obsolete.

Companies operating in sectors across the global economy are actively enabling employees to play. World-renowned innovators such as Google and 3M implement strategies that allow freedom to play and freedom to fail in the workplace. The ethos of companies such as 3M is to provide employees the freedom to pursue their own interests in the hope of promoting and encouraging creativity and innovation. This ethos encourages employees to engage in "playtime" activities that have traditionally been considered a "waste of time" or "unproductive" within business management, such as taking a walk, lying in the sun, or playing pinball (Leher 2012). Organizations that feature regularly on Forbes' 100 Best Companies list are those which have a shift in mindset from "workplace" to "playspace" in which the creative processes of innovation are highly valued and invite passion and enthusiasm into the business (Meyer 2010). A study found that play and fun in the workplace increases productivity, job satisfaction, innovation, morale, and efficiency while reducing absenteeism, stress, frustration, and illness (Pelucchete, Harland, and Karl, 2005). Other researchers have all identified a relationship between fun at work and employees' experiences of positive affect, associated with improved individual and organisational outcomes (Flugge, 2008; Karl & Petchulette, 2006; Tews, Michel, Xu, & Drost, 2015; and Plester & Hutchison, 2016). Perhaps in time education policy makers and practitioners will share in global commerce's recognition that it is the freely chosen and personally directed nature of play that will, in the words of Auserwald (2012, 21) bring "coming prosperity to the world."

CONCLUSION

IN THIS CHAPTER we've aligned resilience with the principles of self-active play. This ultimately leads to and heightens a sense of well-being as a way of supporting healthy growth and development. Finland provides an example of how a culture of respect for play impacts educational beliefs, values, and practices. Play is deeply embedded within the educational system and is a daily expectation fostered by families, children, and teachers. Self-active play serves as a strong play advocacy strategy. Michael Patte shares an example of how a community comes together to provide the children with an opportunity to engage in open-ended free play. In Michael Wragg's work we see the long term negative effect of the absence of free play on children's development, and impairment of success in future job opportunities.

CONCLUSION

THROUGHOUT THE BOOK we've shared our insights based on years of experience using self-active play with children and adults. Through careful examination and analysis of the reflective journals, interviews, and focus groups we've chronicled the impact of self-active play and built a clearer understanding of its importance to human development. Our hope is that you, too, will use self-active play as a tool for sharing the depth and significance of play across the human lifespan.

Play and reflect. The first recommendation we leave you with would be to find time in your own life to freely play with open-ended materials, such as Dr. Drew's Discovery Blocks, rocks, colored tops, pinecones, or small sticks collected from a walk in the woods. It is through the adult's own play experience, a time of creative contemplation, that nourishes the body, mind and soul. The play experience builds resilience, determination, and the deep conviction of a play advocate. Reflect on what happened in your play journal, if you don't mind. Draw, doodle, or write about the thoughts and feelings you had as you played and afterward.

Another recommendation would be to help families develop a deeper sense of the importance of play for family life. The teacher provides parents with similar play experiences for the family. Use self-active play experiences for Open House, Meet the Teacher Nights or 30 minute morning Parent Workshops for parents after they drop their children off. Through the play experience, parents can develop a clearer understanding of what happens when children are given open-ended materials and the time to wonder. In that play experience, parents also develop sufficient skill to play again this way at home with their children.

Our final recommendation would be to join in the WORLD WIDE movement supporting play in the lives of children, as part of this movement embrace self-active education. Other national organizations are involved in supporting play and meeting the urgent need for children to have with time and resources for play. Such organizations as the National Association for the Education of Young Children (NAEYC), Play, Policy & Practice Interest Forum of NAEYC, Defending the Early Years (DEY), The Association for the Study of Play (TASP), the Alliance for Childhood and The Alliance for Self Directed Education all provide support and encouragement to teachers as well as parents to understand and practice play. For instance, the American Academy of Pediatrics (AAP) describes specific recommendations for parents on how to use play as a tool to meet development milestones in children from birth through age six. In the Appendix section of the book we have included multiple resources to encourage and support teachers as they develop, practice and apply the Principles of Self-Active Education in their own professional practices.

We've provided a solid connection between self-active play and research from the fields of sociology and psychology, as well as education. We clarified the significance of using high-quality, open-ended materials that support the creative healing process by stimulating the imagination and origination requiring players to interact with the materials sensorily. We outlined sources for materials and the potential for partnering with community businesses as material donors.

We expanded the scope of self-active play beyond the educational setting. We looked at how self-active play provided a context in which older adults could interact together and how self-active play served as a method for improving quality-of-life factors. We shared the impact self-active play had in a grief center where children and adults suffered from a sudden death in their family. As noted by Thomas Henricks, "If play has a legacy, it is its continuing challenge to people of every age to express themselves openly and considerately in the widest human context." (p.227).

Self-active play education *is* the hopeful advocacy strategy, or master plan. It is in and through the play experience that adults spontaneously reconnect with play memories of their own childhood. Or perhaps they connect their direct play experience to insights about children or others. Self-active play encourages and supports the player's imagination to wonder, connect, and reveal deep understanding. It gives the play advocate a profound place from which true passion arises. This play passion propels advocates to do good work by energizing them, providing profound understanding and the knowledge base to answer skeptics' questions. It begins with a spark: "just touch the materials, fiddle a little while and see what bubbles to the surface." Just a touch, some quiet music in the background, some unusual, intriguing materials, and the opportunity to play.

APPENDICES

Supports in the pursuit of play for all:

1. *Institute for Self Active Education*
   http://www.isaeplay.org/

2. *Dr. Drews Toys, Inc.*
   http://www.drdrewsblocks.com

3. *Reusable Resources Association*
   https://www.reuseresources.org

4. *Reusable Resources Adventure Center*
   https://reusecenterbrevard.org

5. *National Association for the Education of Young Children: https://www.naeyc.org/*

6. *The Association for the Study of Play*
   http://www.tasplay.org/

7. *The Alliance for Childhood*
   http://www.allianceforchildhood.org/

8. *Defending the Early Years*
   https://www.deyproject.org/

9. *International Association for the Child's Right to Play*
   http://ipaworld.org/

10. *International Council for Children's Play*
    http://www.iccp-play.org/index.html

11. *National Institute for Play*
    http://www.nifplay.org/

12. *The Strong*
    http://www.museumofplay.org

Checklists for Self-Active Play Sessions

Individual *Self-Active Play Experience:*

1. *Procure open-ended materials - solicit help from businesses within your community.*

2. *Find time to set aside for playing.*

3. *Find a quiet space without interruptions.*

4. *Play soft instrumental music, like Michael Jones.*

5. *Touch the materials, explore patterns or ways of arranging them and wonder.*

6. *Give yourself 15-30 minutes.*

7. *Take a moment after you are done to contemplate your play experience.*

8. *Journal about the experience; what happened, what thoughts or feelings arose?*

Group *Self-Active Play Experience: (partner or small groups)*

1. *Secure a large number of materials that enable each individual to have their own set of materials in abundance for the solo play.*

2. *Assure that there is enough space in the room to allow a 4 by 4 square area per player on the floor, or table top play can be used for smaller spaces.*

3. *Set up the music so it is easily heard throughout the room.*

4. *Be sure to have journal sheets, notebooks or some way of capturing the experience of the players.*

5. *Be sure to have photography equipment ready to capture the play to support reflection.*

6. *Arrange the materials around the room assuring that different textures, colors and shapes of materials are balanced throughout the room.*

7. *Give a brief introduction ensuring there is ample time for the play; remember the play and reflection is the most important part of the experience.*

8. *Give a 2 minute warning after approximately 25-30 minutes.*

9. *Ask the players to reflect on their experience: written words, drawings, and opportunity to share their experience orally with the group.*

10. *Questions and answers focused on their play experience.*

For additional information on the details of setting up a play workshop see *From Play to Practice: Connecting Teachers' Play to Children's Learning,* Nell, Drew, & Bush (2013), Washington, D.C.

Select Videos from the
Walter Drew YouTube Channel

- *2021 Play with Purpose 9:33*
  https://drive.google.com/file/d/1JG9l8u52Ha2dxn-VH_6UZlNwRUozPqBwd/view?usp=sharing

- *2020 FLAEYC PLAY Chapter: Take Ten and Play, Florida Association for the Education of Young Children (FLAEYC) 8:36.*
  https://youtu.be/AMJBnwKWECQ

- *2020 Kinderoo Silent Solitary Play 4:50*
  https://youtu.be/Jwmx6gux7ao

- *2020 Kinderoo Play with Paints 3:39*
  https://youtu.be/96rCMZmbT8A

- *2019 The Play Experience: National Association for the Education of Young Children (NAEYC) 2:00*
  https://youtu.be/QfLDyDED36A 2:00

- *2017 Exciting the Art Spirit: Play with Paints 10:40*
  https://youtu.be/qSByQ1BcTOo
  Temple Beth Shalom, Needham, MA

- *2016 Playing with Paints with Dr. Walter Drew (Part 1 - Silent Solo Play) 5:58*
  https://youtu.be/ok4_2wG_bFI

- *2016 Playing with Paints with Dr. Walter Drew (Part 2 – Solo & Collaborative painting) 9:06*
  https://youtu.be/VdRQV8dHKto

- *2016 Exploring Paints: Iowa AEYC Play Coaches 3:39*
  https://youtu.be/BMoTO_AGZ_s

- *2016 United Way Family Play with Dr. Drew's Blocks 5:31*
  https://youtu.be/hE__E5a7bKk

- *2015 Cultivating Creativity in Young Children 13:15*
  https://youtu.be/iTFNumCCAwk

- *2015 Brevard After School "Discovery Learning"*
  Part 1 - Solo Play 4:03
  http://youtu.be/nkHQQIe6lXA

- *2015 Brevard After School "Discovery Learning"*
  Part 2 – Team Building 5:17
  http://youtu.be/1qWzMNl58yc

- *2014 Teaching Young Children: Silent Solo Play with*
  Open-ended Materials 14:58
  http://youtu.be/HZk2UGVt9zo

- *2012 Play Workshop with Dr. Walter Drew, Ed.D. 1:15*
  www.youtube.com/watch?v=xgmnBLCKQrw

- *2010 "Hands, Heart & Mind" North Florida AEYC 4:52*
  http://www.youtube.com/watch?v=rwMjvPP6JNQ

- *2006 The Positive Power of Play, Early Learning*
  Coalition of Southwest Florida. 15:30
  https://youtu.be/uGh6MldtOyg

- *1995 Boston Recycle Center #1 "Hands. Heart & Mind" 10:11*
  http://www.youtube.com/watch?v=Elg9KeEXBMA

- *1995 The Recycle Center #2 "Hands, Heart, & Mind" 19:33*
  http://youtu.be/Al5Vg58hpeo

Journals: • American Journal of Play
• The International Journal of Play
• Journal of Playwork Practice

Videos for View

During the 44th Annual International Conference of The Association for the Study of Play (TASP) Conference in 2018 Dr. Thomas Henricks and Dr. Peter Gray gave keynotes speeches and their links to each of the speeches are below:

- *The TASP Distinguished Theorist Lecture: Dr. Thomas Henricks Keynote: "What we "realize" when we play: Selves, relationships, meanings - and other matters?" https://youtu.be/k_YNbMTj8TY 2018. 1:04:47*

- *The Brian Sutton Smith Memorial Lecture: Dr. Peter Gray: "The Promise of Play" https://youtu.be/5VsajvrjMCg 2018 1:10:37*

Sources for Materials

The heart of the play experience is dependent on the quality, variety and abundance of the open-ended materials.

- For a list of resource centers where these types of materials can be acquired visit http://www.reuseresources.org.

- There is also a book written to share how to create a Reusable Resource Center in your own community: "How to Create a Reusable Resource Center: A Guide Book for Champions" This book is available through http://www.isaeplay.org/.

- Solicit help throughout your own neighborhoods and community businesses that discard materials and is an available source of free material throughout your community.

BIBLIOGRAPHY

Adger, W. Neil . (2000). Social and Ecological Resilience: Are They Related? *Progress in Human Geography* 24, 347-364.

Bandura, A. (1997). *Self-efficacy: The exercise of control.* New York: Freeman Press.

Basic Education Act 628/1998. Amendments up go to 1136/2010. Downloaded March 19, 2018 from http://www.finlex.fi/en/laki/kaannokset/1998/en19980628.pdf.

Brown, Fraser. (2014). *Play and Playwork: 101 Stories of Children Playing.* Maidenhead: Open University Press.

Brown, Fraser and Webb, Sophie. (2005). Children Without Play, *Journal of Education,* 35: 139-158.

Brown, Stuart, and Christopher Vaughn. (2009). *Play: How it Shapes the Brain, Opens the Imagination, and Invigorates the Soul.* New York: Avery.

Brown, Stuart. *Brain Research.* (2016). Edited by David Elkind. Rifton, NY: Community Products, LLC. Retrieved from https://www.communityplaythings.com/resources/literature/wisdom-of-play.

Butland, Bryony, Jebb, Susan, Kopelman, Peter. (2007). *Tackling obesities: future choices – project report (2nd Ed).* London: Foresight Programme of the Government Office for Science.

CareerBuilder. (2014). *The Shocking Truth About the Skills Gap.* Available at: http://www.careerbuildercommunications.com/pdf/skills-gap-2014.pdf [Accessed March 18 2018].

Carmody, J., Baer, R.A. (2008). *Relationships between mindfulness practice and levels of mindfulness, medical and psychological symptoms and well-being in a mindfulness-based stress reduction program.* Journal of Behavioral Medicine, 31, 23-33. (p. 24).

Center on the Developing Child, Harvard University. *Applying the Science of Child Development in Child Welfare Systems.* Retrieved 10-12-18 from https://developingchild.harvard.edu/resources/inbrief-applying-the-science-of-child-development-in-child-welfare-systems/.

Chalufour, Ingrid & Worth, Karen. (2004). Building structures with young children. St. Paul, MN: Redleaf Press.

Craft, Anna. (2005). *Creativity in schools: Tensions and dilemmas. NY: Routledge Publishing.*

Csikszentmihalyi, Mihaly. (1996). *Creativity: Flow and the Psychology of Discovery and Invention.* NY: Harper Perennial.

Dictionary.com. (2018). Based on the Random House Unabridged Dictionary 2018. S.v. "advocacy" and "resilience." Accessed August 22, 2018. https://www.dictionary.com.

Edwards, Linda C. (1997). *The Creative Arts: A Process Approach for Teachers and Children, 2nd Edition.* Prentice-Hall.

Emerson, Ralph Waldo. (1984). Emerson in His Journals. Edited by Joel Porte. Cambridge, Ma: Harvard University Press.

Erikson, Erik. (1997). *The Life Cycle Completed.* NY: Norton and Company, Inc.

Fisch, Karl. & McLeod, Scott. (2017). *Did You Know? Shift Happens,* Available at: https://shifthappens.wikispaces.com [Accessed: 22 March 2018].

Folke, Carl. (2016). Resilience (Republished). *Ecology and Society* 21(4):44. https://doi.org/10.5751/ES-09088-210444

Frederickson, Barbara. (2006). Unpacking positive emotions: Investigating the seeds of human flourishing, *The Journal of Positive Psychology,* 1:2, 57-59.

Freese, A. (2006). "Reframing One's Teaching: Discovering Our Teacher Selves through Reflection and Inquiry." *Teaching and Teacher Education* 22, 100–19.

Froebel, Friedrich. (2005). *The Education of Man.* Translated by William Nicholas Hailman from original 1826 publication. Mineola, NY: Dover.

Freud, Sigmund. (1905). *Three Essays on the Theory of Sexuality.* Se, 7. Available from https://www.sigmundfreud.net/three-essays-on-the-theory-of-sexuality-pdf-ebook.jsp [Accessed 14 April 2018].

Gmitrova, Vlasta and Gmitrov, Juraj. (2004). The primacy of child-directed pretend play on cognitive competence in a mixed-age environment: possible interpretations, *Early Child Development and Care*, 174:3, 267–279.

Goldhaber, Dan. (2016). In schools, teacher quality matters most: Today's research supports Coleman's findings. *Education Next,* 16 (2). pp. 56-62.

Gray, Peter. (2011). "The special value of children's age-mixed play." *American Journal of Play*. Vol. 3(4), 500–522.

Gray, Peter. (2011). The Decline of Play and the Rise of Psychopathology in Children and Adolescents, *American Journal of Play,* 3:4, 443-463.

Gray, Peter. (2013). *Free to Learn: Why Unleashing the Instinct to Play Will Make Our Children Happier, More Self-Reliant, and Better Students for Life.* NY: Basic Books.

Hammerness, Karen, Ahtianinen, Raisa , & Sahlberg, Pasi. (2017). *Empowered educators in Finland: How high-performing systems shape teacher quality.* San Francisco, CA: Jossey-Bass.

Henricks, Thomas. (2018). "What We 'Realize' When We Play: Selves, Relationships, Meanings—and other matters?" (speech). 44th Annual International Conference of the Association for the Study of Play: Fulfilling the Promise of Play. https://youtu.be/k_YNbMTj8TY

Henricks, Thomas. (2015). *Play and the Human Condition.* Urbana: University of Illinois Press.

Hoelke, Art. (2018). *How Business and Industry Support Creative Workforce Development.* The Association for the Study of Play Conference, Melbourne Beach, FL.

Holling, C. S. (1973). Resilience and stability of ecological systems. Annual Review of Ecology and Systematics 4, 1–23.

Isen, Alice and Reeve, Johnmarshall. (2005). The influence of positive affect on intrinsic and extrinsic motivation: facilitating enjoyment of play, responsible work behaviour and self-control, *Motivation and Emotion*, 29:4, 297-325.

Jaquith, Ann, Mindich, Dan, Wei, Ruth Chung, Darling-Hammond, Linda. (2010). Teacher professional learning in the United States: Case studies of state policies and strategies. Oxford, OH: Learning Forward.

Karl, K Katherine and Peluchette, Joy. (2006). How does workplace fun impact employee perceptions of customer service quality? *Journal of Leadership and Organizational Studies*, 13:2, 2-13.

Katz, Lilian, Evangelou, Demetra, & Hartman, Jeanette Allison (1990). The case for mixed-age groupings in early education. *An ERIC Report, ISBN-0-935989-31-5,* Washington, DC: National Association for the Education of Young Children.

Klein, Rebecca. (2013). China's Education Proposal Could Mean Less Homework For Students. Available at: http://www.huffingtonpost.com/2013/09/03/china-education-regulations_n_3862080.html [Accessed 12 March 2018].

Konner, Melvin. (1975). "Relations among infants and juveniles in comparative perspective." In *Friendship and peer relations*, edited by Michael Lewis & Leonard Rosenblum, 99–129. New York: Wiley.

Leher, Jonah. (2012). *Imagine – How Creativity Works.* New York: Houghton Mifflin Harcourt.

Leichter-Saxby, Juster, & Law. (2012). *Pop-up resource pack*. Retrieved from Pop-Up Adventure Play website: www.popupadventureplay.org

Meyer, Pamela. (2010). *From Workplace to Playspace: Innovating, Learning and Changing Through Dynamic Engagement.* San Francisco: Jossey Bass.

Mezirow, Jack & Taylor, Edward. (2009). Transformative learning theory. In Mezirow, J. and Taylor, E. W. (Eds.), *Transformative learning in practice.* San Francisco: Jossey-Bass.

Milteer, Regina. M. and Ginsburg, Kenneth. (2011). The Importance of Play in Promoting Healthy Child Development and Maintaining Strong Parent-Child Bond: Focus on Children in Poverty. Pediatrics Dec 2011, peds.2011-2953; DOI: 10.1542/peds.2011-2953. Downloaded from http://pediatrics.aappublications.org/ by guest on March 19, 2018.

urshed, Mona, Farrell, Diana, & Barton, Dominic. (2012). ducation to Employment: Designing a System that Works. New York: insey & Company.

Nell, Marcia L., Drew, Walter F., and Bush, Deborah E. (2013). *From Play to Practice: Connecting Teachers' Play to Children's Learning.* Washington, DC: National Association for the Education of Young Children.

Nell, Marcia L., & Drew, Walter F. (2016). "Geriatrics, Aging and Play." *Play & Culture,* vol. 13, Lanham, MD: Hamilton Books.

Nell, Marcia L., Drew, Walter F., Klugman, Edgar, Jones, Elizabeth, Cooper, Renatta, & Prescott, Elizabeth. (2010). "Play across the human life cycle." *Connections,* vol 12 (2), Play, Policy, & Practice Interest Forum of the National Association for the Education of Young Children.

Newman, M. A. (2008). *Transforming presence: The difference that nursing makes.* Philadelphia, PA: F.A. Davis Company.

Pazzanese, Edward. (1999). Families Creating Together: The Spirit of Inclusive Play and Arts Programs. In M. a. Guddemi, *Play In A Changing Society.* Little Rock, AR: Southern Early Childhood Association.

Pelucchette, Joy V., Harland, Lynn, Hall-Indiana, Lynn and Karl, Katherine. (2005). Attitudes Toward Workplace Fun: A Three Sector Comparison, *Journal of Leadership & Organizational Studies* 12:2, 1-17.

Perlstein, Susan. "Elders Share the Arts." *Generations: Journal of the American Society on Aging*, vol. 15, no. 2, 1991, pp. 55–57. JSTOR, www.jstor.org/stable/4487772.8

Pestalozzi, Johann. 1898. How Gertrude Teaches Her Children, Translated by L. E. Holland and F.C. Turner. Syracuse, New York. C. W. Bardeen Publisher, Reprinted London: Forgotten Books.

Piaget, Jean. (1951). *Play, Dreams and Imitation in Childhood.* London: Routledge and Kegan Paul.

Plato. (2017). *The Republic.* Seattle: Amazon Classics.

Playground and Recreation Association of America. (1925). *The normal course in play –Materials for use in the training of playground and recreation workers.* New York: Playground and Recreation Association of America.

Plester, Barbara. and Hutchison, Ann. (2016). Fun times: the relationship between fun and workplace engagement. *Employee Relations,* 38: 3, 332 – 350.

Porte, Joel. (1982). *Emerson in His Journals.* the President and Fellows of Harvard College.

Pressman, Sarah and Cohen, Sheldon. (2005). Does positive affect influence health? *Psychological Bulletin,* 131:6, 925–971.

Richardson, Glenn E. (2002). "The Metatheory Resilience and Resiliency." *Journal of Clinical Psychology* Vol 58(3) p. 307-321.

Roopnarine, Jaipaul., & Bright, J. (1993). "The social individual model: Mixed-age socialization." In Roopnarine, Jaipaul. & Johnson, James. (1993). *Approaches to early childhood education,* 2nd ed, 223–242. New York: Macmillan.

Russ, Sandra. (2003). Play & Creativity Developmental Issues *Scandinavian Journal of Educational Research* 47:3, 291 - 303.

Sahlberg, Pasi. (2015). *Finnish Lessons 2.0: What can the world learn from educational change in Finland?* New York: Teachers College Press.

Sawyer, Keith. (2008). Group genius: The collective power of collaboration. NY: Basic Books.

Sutton-Smith, Brian. (1997). *The Ambiguity of Play.* Cambridge, MA: Harvard University Press.

Sutton-Smith, Brian. (1999). Evolving a Consilience of Play Definitions: Playfully. In *Play and Culture Studies, Play Contexts Revisited,* edited by Stuart Reifel, 2:239–256. Stamford, CT: Ablex.

Tews, Michael, Michel, John, Xu, Shi, Drost, Alex J. (2015). Workplace fun matters ... but what else? *Employee Relations,* 37:2, 248 – 267.

Trkulja, Tania. (2015). Social resilience as a theoretical approach to social sustainability. DOI: 10.7251/DEFEN1501004T Retrieved March 20, 2018.

Whitman, Alden. (1980). "Jean Piaget Dies in Geneva at 84." *New York Times,* September 17. Accessed August 21, 2017 from https://archive. nytimes.com/www.nytimes.com/learning/general/onthisday/ bday/0809.html?module=inline.

Wilson, Frank. (1998). *The Hand: How its use shapes the brain, language, and human culture.* NY: Vintage Books.

World Economic Forum. (2016). The Future of Jobs Employment. Employment, Skills and Workforce Strategy for the Fourth Industrial Revolution, Available at: http://www3.weforum.org/docs/WEF_ Future_of_Jobs.pdf [Accessed 15 March 2018].

Yogman M, Garner A, Hutchinson J, et al; AAP Committee on Psychosocial Aspects of Child and Family Health, AAP Council on Communications and Media, *The Power of Play: A Pediatric Role in Enhancing Development in Young Children.* Pediatrics. (2018); 142(3): e20182058.

Zhao, Yong. (2015). Not Interested in Being #1 Shanghai May Ditch PISA. Available at: http://zhaolearning.com/2014/05/25/not-interested-in- being-1-shanghai-may-ditch-pisa/ [Accessed 12 March 2018].

ABOUT THE AUTHORS

WALTER F. DREW

Walter F. Drew, Ed.D., is a visual artist, renowned designer, researcher and presenter of hands-on play and artmaking experiences that *awaken creativity, strengthen early childhood practice, and generate hope and optimism across the human life span.* That is the mission of the Institute for Self Active Education (ISAE) Walter and his wife Kitty founded together in 1980. Dr. Drew has proudly served as president of The Association for the Study of Play, facilitator of the National Association for the Education of Young Children (NAEYC) Play, Policy and Practice Interest Forum for 27 years, and currently, as facilitator of the Florida Association for the Education of Young Children PLAY Chapter (FLAEYC). *Dr. Drew's Discovery Blocks* were chosen "Best Toy the Year" by the Parent Choice Foundation in 1982. Dr. Drew is the recipient of the 2009 Patricia Monighan Nourot Award and 2018 "Peace Educators Award". Dr. Drew can be contacted at drwalterdrew@gmail.com.

MARCIA L. NELL

Marcia L Nell, Ph.D. is an associate professor emeritus at Millersville University in Millersville, PA, where she taught graduate and undergraduate courses in early childhood education and supervised student teachers. Marcia was the Department Chair for the Early, Middle and Exceptional Education Department. She served as the Director of Research and Professional Development for the Institute for Self Active Education as well as a facilitator for the Play, Policy & Practice Interest Forum of NAEYC. Marcia is co-author of "From Play to Practice: Connecting Teachers Play with Children's Learning" 2013 published by the National Association for the Education of Young Children (NAEYC). Marcia served as the President and is currently serving as the treasurer for The Association for the Study of Play (TASP), which is an international, multidisciplinary group of play scholars. TASP sponsors an annual conference that highlights the newest research in the area of play across species.

Made in the USA
Columbia, SC
08 February 2022